SHEAR ELEGANCE

GIUSEPPE LONGO

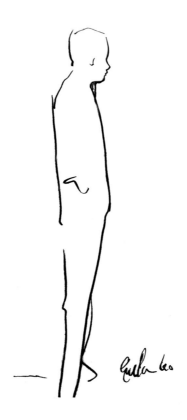

SCHIFFER PUBLISHING

4880 Lower Valley Road · Atglen, PA 19310

Other Schiffer Books on Related Subjects:
An Illustrated History of Hairstyles: 1830–1930, Marian I. Doyle,
ISBN 978-0-7643-1734-7

Classic Beauty: The History of Makeup, Gabriela Hernandez,
ISBN 978-0-7643-5300-0

Designed by Molly Shields
Cover design by Molly Shields
Type set in Guest Check/Cambria

Front cover image: Courtesy of Eve Arnold/Magnum Photos
Back cover image: Courtesy of Dennis Stock/Magnum Photos

ISBN: 978-0-7643-6003-9
Printed in China

Published by Schiffer Publishing, Ltd.
4880 Lower Valley Road
Atglen, PA 19310
Phone: (610) 593-1777; Fax: (610) 593-2002
E-mail: Info@schifferbooks.com
Web: www.schifferbooks.com

For our complete selection of fine books on this and related subjects,
please visit our website at www.schifferbooks.com. You may also
write for a free catalog.

Schiffer Publishing's titles are available at special discounts for
bulk purchases for sales promotions or premiums. Special editions,
including personalized covers, corporate imprints, and excerpts,
can be created in large quantities for special needs. For more
information, contact the publisher.

We are always looking for people to write books on new and
related subjects. If you have an idea for a book, please contact us at
proposals@schifferbooks.com.

By the 1960s, Kenneth had worked with every major fashion
photographer, including Bert Stern for *Vogue*'s "Rooftops" editorial.
In the background, the then Pan Am building is under construction.

Contents

ACKNOWLEDGMENTS

An honorary thank-you to Ms. Victoria Meekins

A special thank-you to Mr. Kiril Hristovski, Mr. Garren,
Ms. Melissa Rivers, Mr. Ken Decker, and Mr. David Wills

Gratitude to all of you who have contributed in your own way:

Her Royal Highness Princess Muna Al-Hussein of Jordan
Her Royal Highness Princess Margriet of the Netherlands
Her Highness Princess Jeet Nabha Khemka of India
Her Highness Begum Saleha Sultan of Bhopal

Mr. Simone Longo
Mr. Roberto Longo
Ms. Grace Mirabella
Ms. Dayle Haddon
Mr. Frank Horvat
Ms. Gloria Vanderbilt
Mr. Christiaan Houtenbos
Ms. Amy Greene
Ms. Sandy Linter
Ms. Babs Simpson
Ms. Mia Fonssagrives-Solow
Ms. Lillian Ross
Ms. China Machado
Ms. Melissa Bancroft
Mr. Maury Hopson
Ms. Jean Shrimpton-Cox
Ms. Suzanne Daché
Ms. Lesley Frowick
Ms. Pilar Crespi
Ms. Kitty D'Alessio
Ms. Gloria Schiff
Ms. Lee Radziwill
Mr. Jeffrey Banks
Ms. Polly Mellen
Mr. Henry Koehler

Mr. Mario Buatta
Ms. Cornelia Guest
Mr. Marton Radkai
Mr. Steven Meisel
Mr. Jeffrey Felner
Ms. Karlys Daly Brown
Ms. Doris Gilbert
Ms. Mary Jane Pool
Ms. Julie Britt
Ms. Lola Finkelstein
Mr. Raffaele Mollica
Mr. Peter Lamas
Ms. Ellen Levine
Mrs. H. G. Rita Eerkes
Mr. Michael Gordon
Ms. Cathy Hardwick
Ms. Denise Duldner
Mr. John D'Orazio
Ms. Lucy Ann Bouwman
Ms. Virginia Montgomery
Mr. Jack Caputo
Mr. Jorge Paris
Ms. Catherine Gigilas
Mr. Julian Tomchin
Mr. Kevin Lee

Mr. Michael Shulman
Mr. Gordon Munro
Ms. Erin Harris
Mr. Joshua Greene
Mr. Bob Gomel
Ms. Julie Hoogland
Mr. Robert Hamilton
Ms. Patricia Fried
Ms. Lauren Wendle
Mr. Andrew Howick
Ms. Maryrose Grossman
Ms. Sabrina Slott-Miller
Ms. Melisa Gosnell
Ms. Deborah Feingold
Mr. Douglas Kirkland
Ms. Francoise Kirkland
Ms. Hannah Adkins
Ms. Sharon Atherley
Ms. April Calahan
Ms. Sarah Kozma
Ms. Pam Huling
Mr. Steven Zelin
Mr. Nick Harvill
Ms. Helena Neufeld

EVENING LOOKS continued

Brown rising, slash of white
Near right, some of the most eloquent lines recorded in this season of crêpe—heavy brown silk, drawn tight under the bosom, slashed open over a white crêpe panel. For the record: strands of coral—oxblood to rare angelskin—stacked at the neckline; hair sleeked to an all-time high. Dress, by Norman Norell, of Staron silk. At Bonwit Teller; Hutzler's; Hudson's; I. Magnin. The coral necklaces, from Tiffany. Another source of coral lighting: Lancôme's new Paquerette 72 lipstick.

Evening narrows, lift of wool.
A long, steady flame of crimson wool, far right—bare, high-waisted, sinuous; its wrap, an enormous wedge of shawl, thick with tzigane fringe. By Adele Simpson, of wool crêpe. Dangly jet-black earrings, by Cadoro. All, at Saks Fifth Avenue. Dress, also at Julius Garfinckel; Rich's; Harzfeld's. The perfect lipstick-pitch: Firelight Red—this new crimson flash, by Dorothy Gray. Coiffures, both pages: towering news by Kenneth Battelle.

BERT STERN

Vogue, October 1962.

Note from the Author

Having built his professional momentum first at Helena Rubinstein's salon and then at Lilly Daché's, Kenneth ascended to unofficial king of the beauty industry by the early 1960s. His roster of prestigious clients swelled as his reputation for making women look fabulous spread first through New York City, then the rest of the country, and eventually around the world. From Jacqueline Kennedy's signature bouffant to Marilyn Monroe's white-blonde mane, through America's political and Hollywood royalty, Kenneth helped cultivate the image of the world's most notable fashion icons—actors, models, socialites, nobility, business executives, industry professionals—the roster of the world's elite was endless.

Humbly, Kenneth never took it all too seriously—to him, hairstyling was a craft, not the art form that others revered it as. Whenever he was told to write a book and tell his story, his answer was "Nobody cares." Despite this, however, he managed to become a religious figure to many luminaries; what started as a trendy fling evolved into a legendary love affair.

At the height of the Kenneth Salon in New York City—a mecca of true elegance—it employed a staff of 140 people. Some referred to it as an institution, others as a palace, but it truly was a miniature universe that attracted the best. His gravitational pull wasn't just with clients, but also outstanding industry talent that later moved on to open their own salons or blaze their paths to become experts in their field.

For this reason alone, it would take another book to respectfully and deservingly mention everyone who was employed at the Kenneth Salon. In order to avoid omitting someone's name, I solely focused on Kenneth's grand career. As Kenneth once said in an interview, "If it were not for my staff, I would not be here today. The people I work with are crucial."

For the past seven years, beset by obstacles while relentlessly searching for Kenneth's photographs as well as inner circle, I have worked to put this book together. It has been a passion project and an opportunity to live another life—another era. I, too, am indebted to Kenneth, for even in his absence, he has given me more than he will ever know. I was an admirer then, and I'm a disciple now.

I strongly encourage using Google throughout the book to research every name that surfaces—one cannot fully grasp the power and notoriety of Kenneth until one understands who visited the salon on a daily basis. It would be almost shocking for anyone working in the beauty industry, specifically with hair, not to know who Kenneth Battelle was.

For ten years, I was fortunate to have been a small part of the Kenneth Salon at the Waldorf Astoria Hotel—by then in its second incarnation and gradually moving toward its end. It had become my frequent escape from my monotonous corporate job, my sanctuary of silence in the urban jungle. I would visit and have coffee. It felt like home. I felt as if I had become an honorary family member.

While in preliminary talks to write his book together, Kenneth, sadly, passed away just before we were to start. I was heartbroken. When I had first approached him about writing his story, I had twice handwritten the same note, sending him the version that I thought was worthy of an authority on elegance who had an eye for beauty. For my personal files, I had saved the second one.

This book has been nothing but an unbelievable and incredible personal voyage.

From my desk, to your library . . .

Mr. Battelle—

I hope you will give me the honor to embark on this journey with you: to preserve history, elegance, and most importantly your legacy.

With much admiration,

"Celebrity to the Stars"

"the Svengali of the Silver Scissors"

"the Secretary of Grooming"

"the Rembrandt of the Ringlets"

"the Picasso of Coiffure"

"the Herod of Hairdressers"

"a diplomat"

"an artist with scissors"

"the artist every woman dreams of just one appointment with"

"that famous wizard of witchery"

—Kenneth's various titles via the press

MELISSA RIVERS STORYTELLS

Mr. Kenneth.

That's what I called him. That's what we all called the most famous hairstylist in twentieth-century New York—never just Kenneth or Ken or even Mr. Battelle. I guess in hindsight that is exactly who he was: formal and intimate, serious yet playful, elegant but genuine. Mr. Kenneth was an endless study in perfect contradictions. And that's what made him a unique and cherished part of my family's life.

As a little girl, I would go with my mother to Mr. Kenneth's salon, located in a big, imposing townhouse located in midtown Manhattan. I remember walking in and thinking that it was so dark—decorated richly with big-flowered, chintz-padded walls on a commanding black background. In contrast, I can still see the kind smiles of Mr. Jack, the greeter, and the ladies working behind the front desk. I also remember thinking that Mr. Kenneth's staff offered the best candy in the world, which always brightened my day. Once inside the salon, you immediately felt the warmth and tenderness set against lavish sumptuousness, which was Mr. Kenneth's stock in trade.

Soon we'd ascend the big, wide staircase to Mr. Kenneth's private salon. It must have felt humbling to know that the best of the best of New York society trudged up these same steps and into Mr. Kenneth's inner sanctum for him to work his magic. It was a special treat to get an appointment at the salon, and a very big deal if he did your hair himself. This privilege, however, was totally lost on kindergarten-age me. What was not lost were the delicious tea sandwiches Mr. Kenneth had waiting up those stairs. What can I say? I was a child, so sweets and food were definitely the way to my heart.

The public side of Mr. Kenneth was widely known, and he just might have been our first celebrity stylist thanks to his remarkable clientele. Being styled by Mr.

Kenneth meant that although you may have arrived disheveled, you truly had "arrived."

My mother was fortunate enough not only to be a client of Mr. Kenneth's but also to be one of his best friends. And that is the Mr. Kenneth whom I remember best. Under his stern, soaring exterior was kindheartedness and a great sense of humor. At the lowest point in my mother's life, following the suicide of my father, Mr. Kenneth became her steadfast rock.

In turn, it became my mother's mission to try to make the refined Mr. Kenneth break with laughter. He fought hard not to react to what she was saying or doing most of the time. He'd simply reply, "Now, Joan, is this really necessary?" The admonishment, of course, only egged my mother on to bigger, crazier antics and practical jokes.

At one point, my mother went so far as to redecorate the lobby of Mr. Kenneth's apartment building in the middle of the night. She chose his service in the US Navy as inspiration and had a portrait of him as a sailor painted and hung on the wall. Instead of a straight, formal rendering, passersby saw Mr. Kenneth with a jaunty sailor's cap on his head, garish tattoos on his arms, and a flamboyant parrot perched on his shoulder. And in a perfect retort, Mr. Kenneth did not even so much as acknowledge her handiwork. That, to the two of them, was the best part of the whole, silly caper.

In keeping with his professional artistry, Mr. Kenneth was an extraordinary gardener. He created the most beautiful vistas at his farm, which were special to him and to anyone who was lucky enough to see them. His country home was his private retreat, and even fewer were allowed inside that cloistered world. My mother was fortunate enough to be one of the people allowed to see Mr. Kenneth in his happiest place. It was there one weekend that my mother and

Mr. Kenneth decided that when they got old and crotchety, they would open a teahouse together. Instead of serving delicious Earl Grey, scones, and clotted cream, their mission was simply to be mean to the clients who dared to enter their fine establishment. For the life of me I cannot remember the name of their imaginary endeavor, but it was something along the lines of "Grumpy & Grumpier's."

Toward the end of his life, and through many hardships, Mr. Kenneth never lost his poise. Even in the hospital, Mr. Kenneth was composed and dignified. He was never unkempt. He never let on how much he was hurting. He wanted to be remembered as the Gentleman (capital *G*) he was, who did not suffer fools lightly. And despite his best efforts, my mother continued to play tricks on him in order to make him laugh.

The passing of Mr. Kenneth in 2013 was a great loss to my family. It is impossible for me to sum up who Mr. Kenneth was, but here's a shot: He was a tastemaker, an impresario, an artiste, and a trusted confidant. And he was everything anyone could wish for in a friend.

I understand how fortunate I was to see into that beautiful world at the top of the stairs, and to witness and experience the mind and soul of one of the most magnificent artists of our time. I also know how lucky I was to call him a friend. Finally, I realize how much he is missed by so many others whose lives, and hair, he touched.

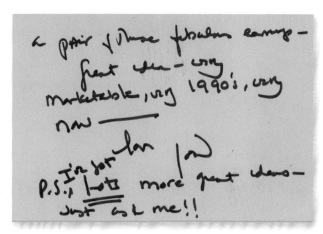

"Dear Dandy Kenneth—
Here's a great idea—For every customer who spends over $101.00, they get a pair of these fabulous earrings—great idea—very marketable, very 1990's, very now.
Love, Joan

P.S. I've got lots more great ideas—just ask me!!"

A Few Words from Garren

I never realized the parallel that I had with Kenneth until I started thinking of my career and the influence he had on it. It's interesting because it was right down to the end when he closed the salon at the Waldorf Astoria—I felt the same when I lost my salon at the Sherry-Netherland. I also realized that I even had a townhouse in a way; we both worked for Glemby International, which is where I met him, and we both came from western New York. I was on Fifth Avenue, he was off Fifth Avenue. He went by his first name only, and that's why I went by mine. It's almost eerie because it's like I tried to copy his whole life, but I did it my way.

Growing up, when I was thirteen years old, I would be looking through the fashion magazines since my mother was very much into them. We were in a little house in Niagara Falls, and we always had *Harper's Bazaar* and *Vogue*. When it became Camelot time, it was all about the Kennedys. I got to meet them at the airport when they came to Niagara Falls during the campaign, and we shook their hands. I saw Jacqueline and JFK and I was just in awe.

My first "introduction" to Kenneth happened at a very young age. When I was small, they used to have little booklets in the grocery stores about the size of an iPhone, and there would be hairstyles. Upon opening them, one would read "Hairdo by Kenneth." It would have a picture of a hairdo that he did, and then on the adjacent page, it would explain how to set it. I was a young teenager, and I would look at these as "bibles"— they had one for Kenneth and one for Vidal Sassoon.

First came Kenneth; I was attracted because it was the 1960s and I wanted to know how to do a bouffant and how to create these certain looks. My mother, who was in her thirties, was prematurely gray, so they would do her hair like an elderly lady. I would get my Kenneth booklet out, and I would study the hairstyle. Then I would brush her hair and tease it, making it into a bouffant. I would try to copy what Kenneth had done.

When I went to beauty school, I started honing in on Kenneth and Vidal Sassoon, who I thought was a brilliant counterpart. There was Kenneth, who was doing all the society dames, all the actresses, all these

Empress Farah Pahlavi (*right*) along with Mohammad Reza Pahlavi, king of Iran, meeting Jerome Robbins's Ballets USA team with First Lady Jacqueline Kennedy (*left*). The Kennedys hosted a dinner at the White House in honor of the royals.

glamorous ladies—he was in *Vogue* and in every imaginable magazine. Then there was Vidal Sassoon, who was trying to take the puff out of the hair and create a geometric haircut. I started combining the geometric haircut with the bouffant and experimenting with hair.

After some time, I finally met hairstylist Christiaan at a hair show, and we ended up having dinner. I told him that I wanted to move to New York, and he said, "Well, you should really come to New York. There are some people I'd like for you to meet." He was the one who eventually introduced me to the Finkelstein family, who were the owners of Glemby International. I ended up working in a salon that Glemby owned in Buffalo, New York, that was called Jenss, which was their rendition of Bergdorf Goodman. When I was promoted to a trainer, Glemby was teaching uniformity at all its salons, which were at department stores such

The Kennedys gather in the East Room of the White House to attend a reading after hosting a dinner honoring Nobel Prize laureates.

as Bonwit Teller, Macy's, and Bloomingdale's, and at all these hotels such as the Plaza in New York City and the Drake in Chicago.

One night, I was invited by the Finkelsteins to join them for dinner at the Four Seasons in New York City. The other person who was sitting at the table was Kenneth, which was the first time I met him. And at that point, I was so shy, and he didn't seem the type of person who would want someone to say a lot about him, but that was what got me more interested in what made Kenneth enigmatic. He invited me to go and see his townhouse, which I went to visit.

When I walked in, I was just in awe. I was in fantasyland. There were all these ladies sitting on banquets, having lunch, and the telephones were brought to them; they would be talking on the telephone while getting their hair done. Then you saw all the elite—you saw Babe Paley, you saw this one, you

saw that one, and Jacqueline. I was like, "God, what magic." The interior was just beyond. He also had these mannequin heads, I don't know if they were lost in the fire, with wood-coiled shaving made into hairstyles. They were very sculptural, the kind of styles that you'd see on Elizabeth Taylor going out to one of her big balls, but it was done with wood shavings. I had thought, *This is so contemporary, but so Old World.*

When I moved to New York things clicked so quickly. Ending up at Bergdorf Goodman, I worked briefly under Suga, who had worked for Kenneth. I was the fashion director for Glemby in the 1970s. Kenneth was still in his townhouse, and he had made a comment with the New York State License Board about men's haircuts, that there should be no difference in price between men's, women's, or children's haircuts because it takes the same amount of time. I completely agreed. I had always believed that it takes just as long to cut a man's head of hair or even a child's, since a child is a moving target. I respected him for his opinion when they interviewed him, and I thought, *Yes! It's about time.* For so long, ladies

11

would say, "He's just a guy; he's just my husband. He just wants a quick little haircut." You still have to section it and balance it, and a hairdresser knows how to do it. It's more work than doing a long haircut.

I had the privilege to be working for *Vogue*, and I was working with Polly Mellen, who was the assistant to Diana Vreeland, who in turn was a client of Kenneth's. Kenneth went about his business, and I always remember him saying, "I'm here to service people; I'm not a celebrity." The statement always stuck with me, that we're in a service business. In today's world, it's about the hairdresser thinking they're the celebrity and people should pay homage to them. It was vice versa in Kenneth's day, and it's still in my mind. I'm honored to have people who want to come sit in my chair.

As that parallel was happening, Kenneth had become older, and he wasn't raising his prices. He made a comment about how much people charge, and I was one of them that he made the comment about. I laughed because I said, "Well, I did start there, but I'm now one of the men of the moment along with John Sahag and Christiaan."

What he had for the moment, I was getting twenty to thirty years later; it's Garren that's in the magazines and still able to handle his clients. I never forgot that humble approach.

We weren't an Instagram world—we weren't blogging about our clients. I always kept that way of doing business, which kept my clientele, but I would never talk about my clients at a cocktail party. They would be sitting next to me, they would be saying hello, but that was the extent of it.

My parallel with Kenneth also included Avedon, Penn, Parkinson, and some other photographers who had worked with him. Every time I went to Avedon's studio, I saw all the portraits that he did with Kenneth. I remember one time, we were driving and it was the time that Madonna was being a trashy version of Marilyn Monroe. I said to others in the car, "God, I wish I had a Marilyn Monroe. I have a lot of Jacquelines right now. I want to do some celebrities."

About a month or two months later, I got a call from Steven Merisel, who asked if I would be interested in re-creating Madonna for a project. I didn't think twice.

When I started with Madonna, my vision was to style her like Marilyn. We ended up doing the *SEX* book; I had an idea. Steven gave me permission, and Madonna was open to it. I always said Madonna was

like my Marilyn Monroe. She had been doing the cheap version of Marilyn Monroe; it was tacky, and I had said we were going to make her classy. I became Madonna's hairdresser for over fifteen years. On and off, she would go to someone else, but when it came to a big shoot or some change, I would be summoned. I always use the word "summoned" because it's something Kenneth would say, or possibly think. I wanted the respect that I was doing her hair and that I wasn't in her business. Nowadays when you get on with a celebrity or a personality or a singer, you're basically waiting on them hand and foot. I'm not doing that. I come in, do my job, and leave.

In my mind, I was always thinking how Kenneth was able to keep his business going, keep the aesthetic, keep everyone happy, and also have a level of excellence. In fact, I did take over a lot of his clientele when the townhouse burned down in the 1990s, because he went to Eva at the Palace Hotel, and the women didn't like the situation.

Steven Meisel was always obsessed with great hair. My muses were Linda (Evangelista), Kristen (McMenamy), Amber (Valletta), Christy (Turlington), and Naomi (Campbell) and that whole group of great models. We would always do an homage to Kenneth for *Italian Vogue*—I would do his grand, big hairdos. At the time, it wasn't in fashion, but when Steven took the picture he made it in fashion.

Steven booked Kenneth in the early 2000s to do a campaign for Michael Kors; Kenneth styled Kristen McMenamy. Unfortunately, I was in the salon that day, and Steven said he wanted me to come to watch Kenneth at work. I said I didn't think it would be a good idea. I wanted him to work his artistry, and I didn't think it was right for me to be in the background. Kenneth did the hair, and Steven was taking pictures in between while Kenneth was styling, because he was obsessed with the whole idea of how he used a hairpin to comb the hair.

On short hair, he put all the rollers in and then he teased it and he created this huge bouffant. It was just so beautiful. She was wearing Michael Kors, a cashmere sweater and a pair of pants. The next day, I came in because Kenneth had to do something else, and Steven showed me the pictures while saying, "You have to kind of do her like this." And I said, "Sure . . . but please don't mix the pictures up. If you're putting this in *Italian Vogue*, give Kenneth his spotlight. Don't have

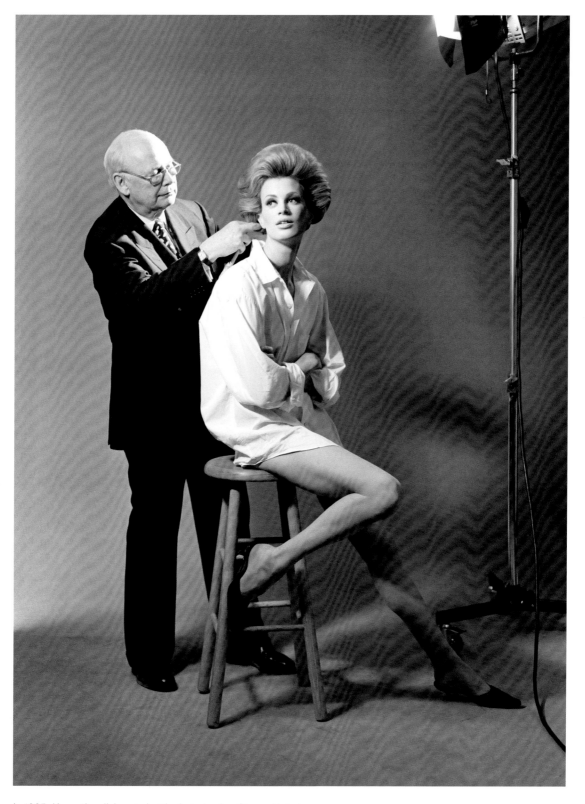

In 1995, Kenneth collaborated with photographer Steven Meisel
and model Kristen McMenamy for *Vogue Italia*.

my page across from his page. Have his styles as a unit and mine as a unit."

He said, "Garren, he put a fall on and he used one hairpin." And I said, "Well, because every model in those days was very disciplined. They didn't flop themselves on the floor. You were put in position." Steven said, "Well, my girls are that disciplined." I said, "They are, but they're not like those days." I ended up doing Kenneth's version. The next day, Kenneth did Amber. Then the following day, I did Amber. He wanted Amber's hair with the fall, so I put the fall on Amber, and it kind of looked similar. I was so happy for Kenneth that he had gotten to do a photo shoot. He worked his magic so quickly. Steven said, "I guess once you really have it, you have it. You don't lose it." Kenneth just knew what to do. That was a great moment in my career.

I've always kept him in my mind. In my salons I always had a dress code. I did not want the staff to stand out as being too cool, I wanted the client to be the most important person in the room. We had leopard robes designed by Ana Sui. When I went to Henri Bendels, I didn't realize that I was in a townhouse. I didn't really do it contemporary. I did it modern, but I also did it like a dressing room in a big ship, which was very elegant. I had a small space, which was understated elegance. It was made with the most beautiful woods and limestone, and the lighting was perfect.

I left that space after fourteen years, and I built a salon at the Sherry-Netherland, which I made like an art gallery. That was my baby. When we were forced to close, Kenneth closed his doors at the same time! I closed January 1 and he closed a couple of weeks after. Writers were calling to do stories about the end of the grand salons. The day of that salon was over . . . unfortunately. And it is over because of the way salons are built now; it's almost like being in warehouses. It's industrial, it's dark, the lighting isn't great, everyone is walking around—they're the personalities; the client is just there because she's there to get a haircut.

What I learned from Kenneth was that the client was the most important person, and that's why I always held him on a pedestal. The closest I got to doing Jacqueline was doing Caroline. She became my client for a couple of years. I got to meet her daughter Tatiana; when she walked in, I said, "She looks exactly like her grandmother." And Caroline said, "I know; she doesn't want to hear it."

I saw Kenneth over at the Waldorf Astoria once; we were having lunch and I stopped by the salon. Kenneth was the Finkelsteins' celebrity flagship; they didn't interfere with him. It was a different time—we were training and teaching, and trying to make all the salons have a certain look, a certain caliber of hairdressing. It was a cut and go, or a cut and blow dry. Kenneth never went into that.

He gave America what Alexandre gave Paris. I admired that he brought so much fashion to the American woman. He broke loose from the tightly coiffed hair and loosened them up and made them sexy. He just knew all about hair. I honor him for that, and I respected him because that's what I gravitated toward. He was my American hero. That's why I think people and hairdressers should know about him— without him, there wouldn't have been that upper class. Even people in the Midwest and all across the country wanted those looks. If it wasn't for him, women wouldn't be using hairpieces and falls. What we do on the set now really started at Kenneth's.

He had his own wig makers, his own people, who would design for the client. The Europeans would come to the United States to go to him. I miss that; it doesn't happen anymore. He had an agreement with Halston that when Halston made a hat for Jacqueline, Kenneth said the hat had to go on the hair and it couldn't destroy the hair. When the hat went off, the hair needed to still be in place. He did create the most famous first lady in the world, who was loved and adored by everyone.

Just weeks before John F. Kennedy would be sworn into office as president of the United States, Kenneth traveled to West Palm Beach, Florida, to style Jacqueline's hair for the sitting with photographer Richard Avedon.

*I believed that hair should be like
fabric—light should pass through it, and you should want to
put your hand in it. I thought of hair as soft, healthy,
lustrous, innocent, and pretty, like a child's.*

—Kenneth

That's silly; it was just my hand! But it was the first time a male hand got the cover of Glamour!
—Kenneth

When Jean Shrimpton came over from England, we grabbed her and had Kenneth do her hair practically every day. Finally, one day he said to me, "Listen, I don't want to complain, but I honestly have done every possible thing to her hair that I can . . . PLEASE don't ask me to do another story on her!"
—Karlys Daly Brown

You know, the most important thing I've learned from him is to look behind everybody's facade. If I saw this man coming into a room, I would avoid him like the plague because he looks so formal. And yet this is my best friend. He's the sweetest, most adorable, funniest child inside that perfectly tailored suit.

—Joan Rivers

My friends in New York, Babe Paley and Slim Hayward,

told me, "You've got to go to Kenneth. He's the best

there is." I was always terrified of haircuts. I didn't

want to end up suddenly with a very short bob. He was

better than they said. He didn't pretend that he was

Mr. Wonderful. He didn't put on any airs. He was

always just a charming and terrific and amusing man

who cut hair better than anyone.

—Lauren Bacall

Photographed by Richard Avedon, style icon Babe Paley, whose
husband was the founder of television and radio network CBS,
became one of Kenneth's most loyal clients.

I have always worked in an isolated way, getting influence from customers. The most interesting education comes from the clients themselves.

—Kenneth

If a girl wore her hair in an upsweep, it looked like she'd managed to get it up there herself with just one hairpin. If you found that hairpin, it would all come tumbling down. I don't want to get involved with the hairdo that's concrete.
—Kenneth

Glamour will always be because it is in people's own minds. If they want it. Glamour is never gone, but descriptions change. There is so much attitude today, which people mistake for glamour. It is a combination of many things: a kind of beauty or a belief in it, a kind of taste or belief in it, a sense of humor, a sense of respect for yourself, a willingness to learn anything. The culmination of these factors in a person is an aura or a feeling a person has about her/himself.

—Kenneth

*There are several hairstyles which I call classic because they have remained—
or will remain—popular for many years: the French Twist, the Chignon, the
Ponytail, and Short Curly hair.*

—Kenneth

Featured in *Vogue*'s April issue in 1962,
Kenneth with model Monique Chevalier
photographed by Bert Stern

One evening in the mid-'60s, I was invited to a vernissage of tempera paintings at Diana Phipps's on Central Park West. In walked Drue Heinz, asking me what I was doing for dinner. I had no plans, so we left in her car along with Marion Javits for the 79th Street Boat Basin. Drue made a call, and a launch arrived to take us to a yacht. The yacht turned out to be Onassis's Christina on its first trip to New York. When we got onboard, people were already having dinner and dancing. Maria Callas made a diva's entrance and took a seat at the bar. I had never before seen a room full of people stand up for a woman. Anyway, I was very happy I went. But the next day in Suzy's column in the Journal-American, *there was a headline: "Pickle Queen Goes to Yacht Party with Hairdresser." I was mortified; I hated it. And I made it a policy not to go out with my clients again. That's not what life is all about. There's an old saying in the publicity field—it doesn't matter what they say about you as long as they spell your name right. I don't believe that. I care very much what they say, and I'd rather not be mentioned at all except in a professional context.*

—Kenneth

I liked Babe Paley. Slim Keith was a hoot. Pamela Harriman and Jeanie Shrimpton were wonderful. I like Lisa Fonssagrives a lot, and I especially loved Kay Kendall. I loved Marilyn. She was very human. Not everybody is.

—Kenneth

Titled as "the World's Greatest Entertainer," actress Judy Garland sits with Kenneth in her dressing room backstage at Carnegie Hall in 1961.

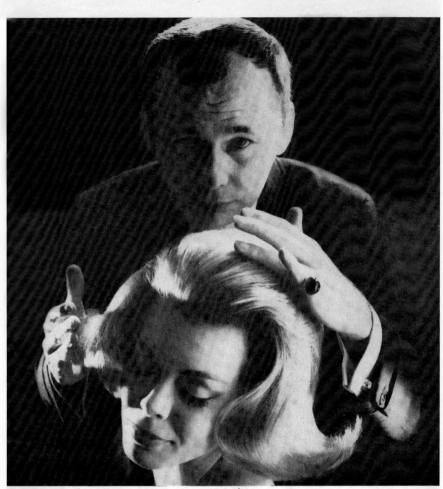

The Mr. Kenneth of New York, award-winning Artistic Director of the elegant Lilly Daché salon

This internationally famous hairdresser tells why you should use a special shampoo if you color or lighten your hair

"When a woman tells me her new hair color makes her feel prettier than ever, I'm delighted," says Mr. Kenneth, whose artistry is acclaimed by many of the world's most important and chic women.

"A good hairdresser, like any artist, strives to achieve beauty in color and form—and to protect that beauty when he achieves it. When I work for a subtle, natural-looking effect in haircoloring, I certainly don't want to see that effect spoiled by color wash-out."

We asked Mr. Kenneth how *he* guards against color wash-out. "Frankly," he told us, "until now it was something of a problem. But now there is a very special answer in new Clairol shampoo, because it is colorfast."

This new colorfast shampoo comes in two special formulas. Clairol® Blue—for lightened and toned hair—guards all light delicate blonde shades. Clairol Green—for tint and lasting-rinse users—guards all red, brown and black shades.

As you might expect, a shampoo fine and gentle enough for colored or lightened hair is marvelous for *all* shampooing. Many women who do *not* use haircoloring use Clairol shampoo simply because it makes their hair shine and feel silky.

Clairol shampoos have been tested and recommended in leading beauty salons here and abroad. Now also available at fine cosmetic counters.

BLUE for blondes

GREEN for everyone else

Kenneth is a kind of hair psychiatrist who not only changes women's looks but their lives and careers.

—Vogue magazine

Airports are quite possibly the windiest places in the world. Remember that your haircut should be one which, when the wind blows through it, a few whisks of your brush and it looks good again. In your life as a stewardess, avoid "evening hairdos"; elaborate styles do not complement your uniforms, which are very graphic. Keep your hairstyles simple and comfortable to work in.

—Kenneth addressing the American Airlines team

I had started doing Marilyn right after Some Like It Hot, *and really, of all my steady clients, Marilyn was the one who was truly my friend. . . . Of course she kept me waiting—to know her was to wait. For three or four hours sometimes—a split second for every hair on her head. But I counted on it, and I allowed for it—and I never minded. Just before she died, she called me from a pay phone. She said she was on the highway somewhere, driving around, and that she just wanted to hear my voice. All in that breathy, little-girl tone she had. But you know something, Jackie talked softer than Marilyn.*

—Kenneth

I defy a woman to wear a Courrèges

without a really great makeup and hairdo.

—Kenneth

Kenneth was a wonderful man, and so many people, the most attractive women, counted on him completely.
—**Lee Radziwill**

I just think about what Halston told me a long
time ago: "You're famous because of your
clients, not because of you."
—Kenneth

He was such a gentleman, suit and tie. He tamed my curls and made me look like I could totally fit in with all the fabulous ladies. He was the most dignified and a legend in his own time.

—Yasmine Sokal (Guenancia)

I think that Kenneth was a great talent and a very nice man.

—China Machado

In 1958, Kenneth styled the hair of China Machado, one of the greatest models in fashion history, for this iconic photograph with Richard Avedon.

KATHARINE HEPBURN, below, as "Coco," was his inspiration when Kenneth went wiggy. He adjusts his "The Surf," one of his four Put-Ons in synthetics, on Barbara Davis, right photo.

Kenneth Goes Coco

By Mildred Hamilton

When Katharine Hepburn asked Kenneth to style her hair for her Broadway show "Coco," he cut a classic page boy chin-length style with bangs.

"However, she washes it herself and rolls it up on the paper curlers she's had forever," said Kenneth, the nation's No. 1 man in hair, as he took a beauty break at I. Magnin yesterday.

Everybody was so pleased with the Hepburn look he decided to launch a new wig line with "Coco" as the inspiration for his first design. He has added "Feathers," a short wig with waves and swirls at the ends, "The Surf," short and straight and ear-tip, and "His 'N Hers," short and curly on top, long and shaggy at back and sides and extra adapted for matching and sharing.

Kenneth, whose East 54th St. salon in New York has influenced coifs coast-to-coast, sees wigs as an extension of his total beauty concept and also as "the hats of the '70s."

"They make a fashion statement. They give a woman a new look quickly — a mood change, a costume match, an enhancement," he said. "I call them my Put-Ons."

The unusually calm and congenial beauty expert is irked about today's tendency to ridicule a President who may or may not color his sideburns. "No, I've never been called to do his hair, but all looks are an illusion and I favor discretion in preserving that illusion.

"I don't think we have to say that we are wearing wigs, we had face lifts, or we have lightened the color of our hair. Anything anyone does to make himself or herself feel more attractive or interesting is fine.

"Ever since Cleopatra and Queen Elizabeth I — who reportedly had 177 wigs — people have been doing things to themselves to be more attractive. We are essentially remembered by how we look."

There will be changes, of course, he noted, "and even ecology has affected this. Beauty will take on a personal meaning. Certainly makeup will be worn but to enhance, not cover the skin. The emphasis will be on good skin, on good hair rather than cosmetics and hair styles."

For today's look he likes the layered cuts that are short and curly on top and long and shaggy at sides and back. "These can be set, or blown dry. What you do to it depends on how you feel that day."

He styled Lauren Bacall's coiffure for "Applause" on that premise. "I've cut her hair for years and she was all one length but the vigorous dancing in the show caused her hair to cover her face. Now she still has length but layering creates a soft, wavy, very pretty look."

He will continue to appear in his own scanty locks. "This mixture of beige and gray is a freaky color to match, and also I have so little hair that it was too much of a shock when I tried on a wig." However, he is pleased other men are eager to wear Kenneth wigs.

All made of wash and wear modacrylic fibers, his wigs and wig accessories range in price from $9 for a brace of braids to $45 for the Hepburn type hair. With his cosmetics and hair care products, they are at I. Magnin.

In 1969, Katharine Hepburn starred in her only stage musical—*Coco*. Loathing and voicing her disdain for having to wear wigs for her performance, she was sent to Kenneth by the producers of the Broadway show. She went up to his private office on the 5th floor at 54th Street, and after introducing each other, he asked her what was the problem. Answering that she refused to wear wigs, Katharine explained that she felt they were keeping her away from the audience because she could not use her body the way she wanted to; they were confining and limiting.

Kenneth had kindly asked her to take off her hat, which revealed her hair pulled up into a little top knot that she had done herself. Observing her hair, he shared that he had a feeling that the outside of her hair had been bleached by the sun and darkened, but it was probably a more natural color when let down. Not only sensing her frustration, but also that she was a private person who wouldn't be pleased if he touched her, Kenneth asked her to take down her hair herself. She obeyed.

"You see, it's brown and it looks perfectly fine. All you have to do is trim a little and put in the curlers . . ." At that moment, for the first time, Kenneth touched Katharine Hepburn to show her how to use the curlers that would make her hair look like Coco Chanel. It would become her first professional haircut since 1955.

I went to Kenneth's at Lilly Daché on Lola Finkelstein's recommendation. Then I went to him faithfully every week ever since! Kenneth was an artist; he was wonderful. I wrote a little piece on Kenneth for "The Talk of the Town."
—Lillian Ross

Kenneth Talks About Your Hair

Kenneth is probably the most famous hairdresser today, and, in his luxurious salon housed in a five-story Edwardian mansion in New York, he styles some of the best-known heads in the world. To have a hairdo by Kenneth is like wearing clothes by Dior or Norell — it's high fashion, it's pretty, it's ladylike and it's expensive.

As a man who doesn't believe in gimmick hair styles, he's been making headlines since he designed the bouffant coiffure for Jackie Kennedy a few years back. Though a quiet and courteous man, Kenneth has very definite opinions which he will tell you on the following pages. — JOAN RATTNER

For the opening of his new salon, Kenneth has created the "Shell" cut. Inspired by the shapes and contours of seashells.

—A 1963 press release for the Kenneth Salon

I remember Kenneth as one of the most elegant men in the business. He had a way about him that was very elevated, bringing elegance and grace with him when he worked. He was devoted to creating beauty, and we were all swept up in his beautiful vision. He was a gentleman apart in this business!

—Dayle Haddon

Hair is a living thing. I like when somebody sits down in the chair and they're
not particularly happy or they wished they looked better. By the time they
leave, they do. And that's very satisfying.

—Kenneth

Like the great name designers in fashion, beauty has its great names in hairdressing . . . it is Kenneth, who appears at the very top of the Beauty Establishment.

—Edith Head

The cut is every bit as important in hair styling

as in a Balenciaga suit.

—Kenneth

In 1965, Kenneth held an unforgettable "Happening" for the press, mostly fashion editors from out of town. Andy Warhol had been there; Sally Kirkland jumped out of a cake in a bikini. The evening included parading musicians, a film by Warhol of a man eating a mushroom, which lasted an hour, and poetry readings by a poet. The ladies, stunned by what they had just experienced, tried making sense of it all.

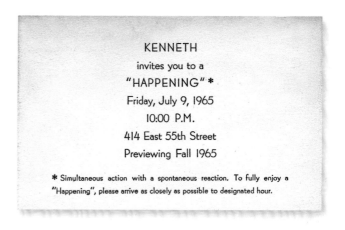

KENNETH
invites you to a
"HAPPENING" *
Friday, July 9, 1965
10:00 P.M.
414 East 55th Street
Previewing Fall 1965

* Simultaneous action with a spontaneous reaction. To fully enjoy a "Happening", please arrive as closely as possible to designated hour.

Kenneth would go on tour for his cosmetics line and give symposiums to dedicated followers. Most of the time, travel was done by air, and in those days, the '60s and '70s, one dressed formally to get on a plane.

Whenever Kenneth made appearances at the stores or held events, the cosmetics would sell well. Kenneth was very famous at the time, and ladies around the country respected him and his opinion.

"You know the way he looks at her, and I want him to look at me the same way," Jacqueline Kennedy had said to Kenneth. He replied, "I'll do this with your hair because when it falls forward, he'll be forced to remove it out of your eye." And that's why Kenneth loosely tucked a wisp of hair behind her ear. She would then have her husband's attention. Remarkably, holding his cards close, Kenneth was the person in between the pair, discreetly delivering a message through a hairstyle.

. . . And So It Begins

With a childhood cemented in the Great Depression, Kenneth's story began in Syracuse, New York, on April 19, 1927, when he became the sole son in a household of five children. When Kenneth Everette turned twelve, his father—who successfully worked for the renowned Nettleton Shoe Company—left the family, and Kenneth assumed the task of providing for his mother and four sisters. Limited in options and skills, yet learning to be independent, a young Kenneth earned meager wages after school and during summers in his hometown.

"He grew up in abject poverty," said Joan Rivers, who would one day become one of his closest friends. "He told me he walked on the train tracks to pick up bits of coal to keep his family warm in the winter."

Kenneth rotated odds-and-ends jobs, ranging from operating an elevator in the town's tallest building, to washing dishes or serving coffee at the railroad station, to selling hot dogs and Coke at a baseball stadium. For a period, he was also a stockroom boy in a factory and then a shoe salesman in a national variety store chain called W. T. Grant. He was always open to any possibility—everything from soda jerk to sales clerk. Unbeknown to him at the time, he was building his relentless work ethic that would greatly serve him in his adult career.

An aficionado of movies from an early age, a passion he carried for the rest of his life, he attended the cinema at every chance. He'd draw inspiration from all that flashed across the screen—details he'd later use in business. He also had an affinity for public speaking, including debate groups and drama.

Yearning for a change in pace at seventeen years old, he left high school during his junior year and enlisted in the United States Navy. Fearing that he might get drafted into the army during World War II, he chose to go to sea because he despised military life.

From boot camp at Seneca Lake, Geneva, New York, he transitioned into the medical corps at Bainbridge, Maryland. Not long after starting there, it was realized that Kenneth would not succeed to completion—pricking people with needles was far too distressing. When he was sent to observe an autopsy, he fainted and had to be carried out. Then he was appointed as a medical corpsman to a paraplegic unit, but he soon requested to be rotated to another wing after finding it too upsetting. He was sent to Lido Beach to sell war bonds and document medical records in a naval discharge ward.

Dispatched to the officers' ward, two distinct events happened within hours of starting his new role. His first duty was to give an enema to an admiral's aide, who happened to also have been a silent screen actor with high visibility. The mission was not deemed a success—the patient heaved a vase of flowers at him. Then, without any proper training on how to maneuver the waxing machine, he was asked to shine the floors. Like a fugitive escaping prison, the machine escaped from his hands and rammed right through the wall.

Weeks after World War II ended, Kenneth visited New York City with several of his fellow sailors. Wandering down Park Avenue, he witnessed a moment that seemed out of a film: mere minutes that would plant the first seeds of a grand idea. Noticing a

In 1967, Kenneth decorated model Marisa Berenson with a fury of corkscrew ringlet hairpieces for a *Vogue* photo shoot with famed photographer Irving Penn.

Across from the Greyhound bus terminal in Syracuse, New York, Kenneth began his career in a small salon at the base of the Hilton Hotel. There, he would create the wildly popular "Club Cut."

massive, captivating beige Lincoln Cabriolet turning a nearby corner, which was driven by a uniformed gentleman in matching beige, Kenneth wondered who was in possession of such a scene. The more the car inched forward, the more details he saw. Spoke wheels, spare tire elegantly mounted to the side, sunlight bouncing off the sleek metallic body. Coincidentally, the Lincoln stopped in front of Louis Sherry's imperial restaurant at 300 Park Avenue—fifty years later, Kenneth would have his own salon across the street at the Waldorf Astoria Hotel.

A lady's elegant black satin shoe revealed itself from the car first. Adorned with a resilient diamond buckle, it was soon followed by a seductive leg concealed in black silk stockings. A vision of beauty emerged, with her neatly coiffed hair locked by an unimposing hat and her face shrouded by a thin black veil. She walked toward the restaurant as her skirt sensually embraced her legs. Kenneth couldn't help but stare, carrying the memory with him back to base and proclaiming, "I have just seen why I have got to move to New York City!"

His tenure lasted eighteen months, and once discharged from duty, he was entitled to six months of education via money from the GI Bill. Although initially wanting to be a psychiatrist, he quickly realized it wasn't reasonable—he would not have been able to fund the rest of his studies, and he needed to support his family once again.

"So when I spotted an ad for a beauty school that read 'Earn $100 A Week In 6 Months,' I thought, 'That's for me!'" Kenneth stated. "I had absolutely no idea what I was getting myself into." He continued: "I had enough of piano by that time, and I'm not a painter. But I wanted to get into a creative job, so I signed up for hairdressing."

Conducting his research by writing to *Vogue* magazine, which had an educational department, Kenneth asked the editors, the higher powers of fashion, for recommendations to beauty institutions. Upon receiving an insightful response, "a list that was three miles long" that included schools in New York City, he chose to become a student at Wanamaker Academy of Beauty on East 42nd Street and 5th Avenue because he liked the sound of the name. Kenneth stayed for as long as his various jobs supported him—playing the piano at supper clubs and performing a small part in a very short-lived Broadway show—until returning to Syracuse and continuing his studies at Marinello Academy of Beauty Culture.

"I didn't immediately dislike hairdressing, but I found it very strange. I remember the first time I put my hands through somebody's hair. It felt very weird. I saw it simply as a way of earning money."

His mother, who he said was raised "very Yankee," detested that he had chosen a career in hair. According to her, "red-blooded American boys" didn't do anything artistic.

Kenneth's studies included learning how to give permanents. Although the one without machines was starting to become common in the hair landscape, he learned to do both—with and without machines. A friend's mother visited him one day for a hairstyle, requesting a machine permanent. Once she was hooked up to all the attachments, looking like Medusa, Kenneth was terrified of the machine; he turned it on and walked away. After a few minutes, he looked over to see smoke rising from her head. Shouting for the teacher and dashing toward the chair, he had mistaken her cigarette smoke for her hair frying.

Applying to an open hairdressing position just for the holidays, Kenneth decided it was time to use what he had learned. "I lied about my experience," Kenneth recalled. "Toward the end of the day, I was left alone in a booth with a client who had come from a little town 90 miles away. Little did she know that she was my first victim."

The client had informed Kenneth that her hair tangled easily, so she would need a vinegar rinse before he started. "I couldn't find any vinegar. I took a product that sounded as though it would do the job. When her hair dried, it looked like a plaster of Paris wig. I had to pry each hairpin loose. I had to rub each individual hair. I got through at nine o'clock. Her hair stood out perfectly straight like a cartoon."

The only thing he could tell the client—"I guess it didn't turn out."

"She left! I left! I never came back to the store. I guess she didn't either."

Graduating in 1947, he started working at a three-booth beauty parlor called the Starlet Beauty Bar, which was in proximity to the Greyhound bus terminal. He stayed for two years. Making $30 a week plus tips and a commission after doubling his salary, he soon buried himself in his work with his laser-focused dedication—working over twelve hours a day, six days a week.

"This was great experience. I got to know what a beauty salon was all about. I started reading *Vogue*, *Harper's*, *Glamour*, *Charm*. I studied the hairdos and began getting ideas," Kenneth reminisced.

What at first was an affordable and less trafficked beauty parlor soon had a reason to raise its prices.

"I made up something there called the 'club cut,'" he said. "A Waspy, wavy bob inspired by '30s magazine illustrations. Within six months, we became THE shop in town."

Having gradually grown stifled and disappointed by the local clients who didn't allow him to be creative, Kenneth was ready for whatever was next. "I was afraid to move to New York City in case I didn't make it. I had been there during my time in the service and knew how grand and big it was in comparison to everywhere else. I liked New York City and wanted to be a part of it, but I was fearful. So I took another step and moved to Florida."

Motivated to take his career momentum elsewhere, Kenneth followed the talk of there being money to be made in Florida in October 1949, and eventually landed in the hair salon of the Sorrento Hotel in Miami by January. He couldn't find a worthwhile job, and the hotel was his only option—the experience was horrendous.

"In the forties, Florida was a great place to be, and many people had told me that the streets were paved with gold for hairdressers."

Kenneth quickly learned the opposite, and with great difficulty. The resident hairdressers were not welcoming, fearing the loss of their business with the influx of other hairdressers from the rest of the country coming for the summer season. Due to their concern, state licenses were an obstacle to obtain, but he was able to make it.

He had always been proud, but brusque to mention that he had taken the very first New York State boards, a license that was nearly impossible to earn. Prior to then, licenses had not existed.

"Licenses were designed to protect those already in hairdressing, not to make for better schools or a better industry. It was simply to stop people from traveling from state to state."

The Sunshine State was neither his success story nor his destiny, it seemed, but New York City, which he had initially feared, would change his life forever. After realizing that Florida was not going to offer much of a future, let alone the Sorrento Hotel, Kenneth saved enough money for a one-way ticket on an unscheduled flight to New York City. He arrived on July 1, 1950, with $8 in his pocket, moving in with a friend from Syracuse who lived in a very little apartment in the back of a renovated tenement on 3rd Avenue between Avenue A and Avenue B in Manhattan. Within days, he was hired at the renowned beauty mecca of Helena Rubinstein on 52nd Street and 5th Avenue.

For *Vogue* in 1965, Bert Stern captured British photographer David Bailey bewitched by supermodel Veruschka, whose hair Kenneth had styled.

The Queen of Beauty: Helena Rubinstein

Bright lights, incredible sights—the Big Apple was the most exciting place to be in the country. After landing in New York City, Kenneth focused on finding a job. Aside from Antoine from Saks Fifth Avenue, he had heard of another name.

"The best-known hairdresser at the time was Michel at Helena Rubinstein," Kenneth shared. "I wanted to work for him, but I was afraid to go there. I went to Rubinstein's one day but got stage fright at the door and walked down the street to Elizabeth Arden's."

Kenneth had been in awe of Elizabeth Arden's majestic salon. As part of the interview, they provided him with a model to style her hair. Once finished and after the team of ladies had reviewed his work, the manager told Kenneth that they had a job for him—in the company's salon in Lexington, Kentucky. Furious at the offer, he stormed down the street to Helena Rubinstein's salon and requested an interview.

Before starting, he quickly did his research—he marched through Rubinstein's hallways, lined with about thirty-six rooms, and observed what the resident hairdressers were doing. Terrified, but finally feeling confident that he had an understanding of the Rubinstein look, Kenneth tried to mimic it on the wavy gray hair of the telephone operator they had introduced to him.

"As I was doing her hair, I heard someone explain that Michel never hired anyone with less than five years' experience, preferably with 5th Avenue salons," Kenneth recalled.

When Michel asked him about his prior experience on 5th Avenue, Kenneth lied and mentioned the name of another salon on the street that he had once seen. "By the time I was called in to Michel's office, I had

Elizabeth Arden's greatest competitor, entrepreneur Helena Rubinstein, moved to New York City in 1915 to open her first cosmetics salon. Referring to a rivalry that lasted a lifetime, Madame Rubinstein once stated, "With her packaging and my product, we could have ruled the world."

With homes as impeccable as her taste in art, Helena Rubinstein was a marketing maven. Using it all to her advantage, she befriended artists, loaned her homes for magazine photo shoots, and offered free salon services to industry professionals for credit in print stories.

made up a whole background. I don't know whether he believed me, but he said, 'I like the way the model's hair looks. We'll give you a three-week trial. If we're satisfied, we'll keep you.'"

He had passed the test. Not only was he where he wanted to be, they were also going to pay him $50 a week. Kenneth was deliriously happy.

He ended up staying until 1956, almost six years. Under the authority and watchful eye of hair maestro Michel Kazan, the salon was the institution that taught Kenneth the hair trade.

Ms. Rubinstein, or "Madame" as she was often called, who built an empire that made her one of the richest women in the world, was a shrewd business-woman. Working for her proved to be quite educational. There was no better place to learn the industry. An environment filled with actresses, models, and industry professionals, the salon was an oasis of visible people. There he would hone his hairdressing skills as well as the art of haute coiffure.

Since he was the newest addition to the team, Kenneth was given the outermost booth. The least inviting of the rooms, it was furnished with only the necessities: a mirror, a chair, a sink, and a counter with a few brushes and scissors. On his first day at

work, he did two permanent waves. Being used to making around $0.25 tip, he was elated when one client left him $5 and the other $20. Kenneth noticed with time that Michael Kazan received a lot of attention at the salon; he would do hair consultations. While conversing with the client, he would hold her hair up and pin with his smattering of hairpins, showing somewhat of a hairstyle that the client wanted. Once everyone was satisfied, he would pass the client to another stylist who would then create the finished look.

Being the lowest rung on the ladder, Kenneth received all the clients that no one else wanted in the salon—assistant beauty editors, models, and former employees. Notorious for publicity, Madame Rubinstein gave free salon services to industry professionals in lieu to sometimes receiving magazine credit lines.

"The other hairdressers would do these girls badly, so they wouldn't come back," Kenneth explained. "There were no tips or percentages to be made."

Kenneth didn't care, though. The work ethic instilled in him from his childhood served him well. For several years, in the last booth of the salon, Kenneth practiced his craft and perfected his eye.

While other hairdressers declined, Kenneth accepted assistant editors' requests to prepare models'

Kenneth shared a connection with Joe Eula that blossomed into a friendship, based on a mutual respect for one another's artistic talents. Eula would visit Kenneth at work to draw the happenings of the day.

hair for photo shoots, exposing himself to the magazines, editors, photographers, and the overall process. "I enjoyed them and I became a better hairdresser on those stories [photo shoots]—I got a chance to invent, to be creative."

The only downfall: the Rubinstein salon was credited once the stories were printed in the magazines, not Kenneth. From that experience, Kenneth vowed that if he ever had a salon, the hairdresser styling a sitting would receive the credit. "When I started to do hair sittings for the fashion magazines, Michel's staff was never allowed to get credit lines. We were merely hairdressers from Michel's." As his resentment gradually increased, Kenneth became dissatisfied and restless.

Over time, Kenneth found himself with an eclectic circle of clients. Interestingly so, like him, these clients were becoming more powerful and growing professionally in their industries. Assistant beauty editors became beauty editors, junior professionals became executives, and models went from being in the pages of magazines to becoming cover girls. Further strengthening trust and loyalty, he volunteered to visit clients at their homes to style their hair for any special occasion they were attending that evening. Customers became friends.

One morning in 1954, Kenneth started a long-term friendship with an unknown senator's wife from Boston that would one day evolve into a national sensation. Newlywed Jacqueline Kennedy was staying with her husband's family while he underwent medical examinations at the Cornell University Medical Center. Whenever she was in New York City and her hair needed attention, Jacqueline always visited Lawrence at Rubinstein's. He had styled her hair for her wedding. On that particular day, Lawrence happened to be out with a cold.

"Over the loudspeaker," says Kenneth, "they called me to the desk and said, 'This is Mrs. Kennedy. What's his name is sick. Would you mind...?'"

To Kenneth, Jacqueline was just another client from Boston. Her name didn't mean anything to him. Studying her hair once she was seated in his chair, Kenneth realized that her hairstyle didn't suit her look.

"At the time, Mrs. Kennedy had what was known as the Italian Cut," Kenneth said. "She was a very pretty girl whose hair had a mind of its own. It was too short, layered, and curly for her tall proportions and big

In December 1955, while working for Helena Rubinstein, Kenneth created the perfect braid for style icon Countess Jacqueline de Ribes, who was photographed by Richard Avedon.

(Following) A double-page spread by Richard Avedon in the July 1960 issue of *Harper's Bazaar*.

Comtessa Christina Paolozzi

arrow of herself toward the cup of enigma that is hers alone. Another is bound only by the awareness of her own boundaries—Primavera seeing her own nimbus clear.

T*his is their talisman: in a day where every luxury is easy except that of identity, they possess this ultimate secret. Like their great prototype, they will hold our interest with it, forever.*

Opposite: Fourteen layers of drifted white chiffon, with stole and strapless décolletage marvelously beaded. By Sophie, to order at Saks Fifth Avenue. On all Sphinx pages, hair arranged by Kenneth of Lilly Daché.

bones. I planned to soften the line and the shape, and I suggested she do this by growing her hair longer. I wanted to stretch it out by setting it on big rollers—the only problem is that they did not exist then."

For the longest time, hair was set with pin curls, but the Italian Cut changed that because it required volume. Unfortunately, rollers were rarely seen. Identifying the need, Kenneth had specific rollers created in plastic. Although never confirmed, it was rumored that Kenneth created Lucite hair rollers.

"Everyone in the salon thought I was crazy, but the rollers did the job, and soon I became known around town as someone who did hair a little bit differently," Kenneth said.

Described as several inches of layered hair set on rollers to give volume and then brushed and worn curly, the Italian Cut had been a breakthrough right from the beginning. Hair that had been worn flat for years suddenly had lift. After some time, the style evolved into the Bubble, which was characterized as having the same haircut as the Italian Cut, only set on larger rollers, including the bangs, for a smoother finish. Unintentionally as well as naturally, the Bubble grew longer and morphed into the bouffant, since women were not cutting their hair on a regular basis. Teasing and hair spray grew hair higher and bigger, which gave way to the voluminous beehive.

As word of Jacqueline's new look got around, his idea was seen as revolutionary, and he garnered a gradual increase of attention during the remainder of his tenure at Rubinstein.

Those were the days when hair was frequently permed until it wasn't recognizable anymore. Stationary hairstyles built to last, they were tight frizz lacking luster. Kenneth often compared hair salons to laundromats—ladies were getting "washed and ironed" hair. Jacqueline heeded his advice, and when she returned to New York City, she booked her appointment with Kenneth. Afterward, she alternated between Lawrence and him.

In 1960, for the July issue of *Harper's Bazaar*, Italian noblewoman Marella Agnelli, who was married to Fiat tycoon Gianni Agnelli, was photographed by Richard Avedon. She would become a symbol of elegance and beauty for the rest of her life.

A Millinery Empress: Lilly Daché

Millinery empress Lilly Daché presided over her nine-story emporium at 78 East 56th Street, between Madison Avenue and Park Avenue. A modernist structure that she had built after demolishing two smaller buildings, her kingdom, where she resided in a penthouse on the top floor, made her the most successful milliner in the world. Sharp and business savvy, she was highly respected for her cunning personality and impeccable sense of business.

The ladies who visited Helena Rubinstein's beauty salon would likely buy a hat at Lilly Daché's. Starting in the 1930s, hats were a necessity to a lady's wardrobe. No lady was seen in public without one. It was believed that hats elevated their appearance.

In the 1950s, change started occurring. Until then, hairstyles had not been very attractive. Suddenly, hair, which had been hidden for so many years, was slowly being seen as an accessory of its own. Ladies started to experiment, and they started visiting the beauty parlor two or three times a week to maintain their look. Lilly Daché, having seen the writing on the wall, decided it was time to open a beauty parlor of her own in her building.

When the salon finally opened, one ascended a carpeted grand staircase to the second floor. A rotunda of mirrors on the wall faced with salon chairs and vanities reflected not only any other client sitting in their chair at another station, but also the soft pink and white walls, reminiscent of Eloise at the Plaza Hotel. After all, the first edition of the book by Kay Thompson stated, "My mother knows Lilly Daché." It was spectacular for its time, but it was always vacant since the salon madness hadn't quite caught fame yet.

Wondering how she could garner some attention as well as a clientele, Mrs. Daché consulted two of her favorite models, Gillis MacGill and Melissa (Missy) Bancroft.

"We both told her, 'The salon is beautiful, but you need a hairdresser,'" MacGill said. "And Lilly said, 'Well, then find me a golden boy—a genius of hairdressing!'"

The rest is history; upon the ladies' persistence, Kenneth went to Lilly Daché for an interview in 1956 and shortly after became the style director of the salon and chief hairdresser.

"One night, Gillis took me over and introduced me to Madame Daché. I told her my hopes and aspirations.

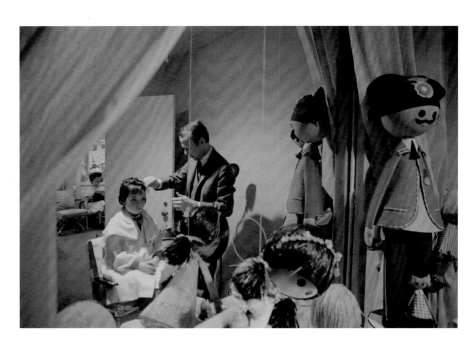

Within her emporium, Lilly Daché created the Doll House Salon, which was where Kenneth styled his littlest clients.

During his tenure at Lilly Daché's salon, Kenneth gained further momentum as news of his talent spread and ladies flocked to book appointments with him.

It was a good move for me. I had more exposure, more opportunity to work with magazines. I developed more confidence in myself as a creative person."

"Now my name appeared on everything I created for the newspapers and magazines. We became the most important salon in New York City and had many famous clients from all over the world."

Like disciples, Jacqueline Kennedy and most of his other powerful clients followed him to his new endeavor. In an unbeknown competitive spirit to win over the ladies, while Mrs. Daché was on the top floors constructing hats, Kenneth was on the bottom floors constructing hair.

Clients walked in and directly into the Daché boutique, followed by the curved receptionist desk behind. Sitting there, as if part of a militia, several

ladies systematically answered the telephone and any inquiries, prepared bills, collected money, and monitored the appointments for each hairdresser. The weekends were known as a time of social affairs, and every Thursday and Friday, on the same day at the same time every week, it was customary for clients to show up to their standing appointment with their preferred hairdresser. The clients, who were only ladies, changed out of their street clothes and into pink cotton robes for their beauty services. Off the main circular salon were a handful of private rooms, each with a chair, sink, and mirror. Models used to walk off the elevators, modeling clothes or hats while clients were having their hair dried or cut.

"I did public relations for Madame Daché in conjunction with her big PR firm run by Eleanor

Lambert," said former publicist Doris Gilbert. "I remember my Daché days because there was interesting millinery as well as hairdressing and beauty. Madame Daché created hats for many stars.

"Kenneth stood out in the work field because he was dedicated and also very fair to clients and editors. He was a hard worker who enjoyed what he did, and did it creatively and often with foresight, getting press-worthy results. He set an example to all, working harder than anyone."

During Fashion Week, then known as Press Week of New York, Doris Gilbert and Kenneth would organize creatively eclectic press events, accommodating those from the industry; press kits and gift bags were given out and attendance was always high.

"One exciting and fun press event was a Fourth of July picnic in a townhouse," remembered Doris. "The food was by Serendipity, and Kenneth balloons were released into the night sky. Another excellent press event featured Rudy the Omelet King, creating all sorts of omelets for guests."

British actress Kay Kendall, a dedicated client of the Elizabeth Arden salon, was "one of the most striking-looking women I've ever seen," Kenneth once said. "A tall, gorgeous clown."

One afternoon in 1957, Gillis MacGill, on her way to Lilly Daché's boutique, happened to run into Kay on 5th Avenue, who had just returned from Hollywood and was rushing to Elizabeth Arden's salon.

A Joe Eula illustration depicting Lilly Daché's salon.

"Kay had just wrapped *Les Girls*, and her hair was dyed that ghastly Technicolor red," said Gillis. "I asked her where she was going, and she said, 'To Elizabeth Arden. I've got to do something about my hair. I look like Danny Kaye in drag!'"

Gillis took her by the arm and led her to Kenneth, who shortened her long hair and darkened it back to its original color, eradicating the shocking crimson. For detail, he added highlights and gave it a soft curl.

"I cut her long hair because so much of it was in bad condition, and toned down the red as near as possible to her own natural brown," Kenneth recalled. Since Kay was very popular, so was her new coif. It even made an appearance in a *Vogue* issue photographed by Irving Penn. It fanned the flames of the flickering fire—people lined up and down the street to get into the salon just to get the Kay Kendall look.

It was around the same time that Babs Simpson went to Kenneth's as a customer. "I was very fond of Kenneth, and we became great friends and we worked together a great deal. I liked what he did; it always had a natural look. Whenever we did a sitting, it looked very contemporary, but it was never so exaggerated that the personality of the model was lost. I think that was what his great talent was—that he was able to give a new look without damaging the person."

Rachel Lambert Mellon, often referred to as Bunny Mellon, who was renowned for her refined taste, impeccable sense of style, and public discretion, starting visiting Kenneth at his salon chair.

"She came just by word of mouth," Kenneth said. "Because somebody had told her I was sympathetic and wouldn't cut her hair too short, and hairdressers had always cut it too short before."

What first started as a standard service relation soon became a lifetime friendship. Both sharing the principle of keeping one's private life out of the public, they also bonded over paintings and gardening. He spent hours beautifying his backyard gardens, and she toiled over redesigning the White House's Rose Garden. They exchanged flowers and planting tips.

He loved perusing the art pieces at Parke-Bernet Galleries, which eventually became the United States' largest auction house. Sometime later, it would be acquired by Sotheby's of London. Very often, he would meet with Babs Simpson on a Saturday in New York and just browse art galleries.

As Kenneth gained momentum at Lilly Daché's, he started attracting more celebrated clients. One day, in a dramatic appearance, Lucille Ball stood at the top of the stairs, looking for Kenneth, and while staring at the maids and other hairstylists around her, demanded, "Where is God?" Rapturous laughter filled the room, including from Kenneth. He thoroughly enjoyed spending time with her, finding her pleasant and so relaxed. During one of her appointments, his mischievous spirit decided to play a trick. Starting with his regular routine of cut, set, and dry, he plotted silently. "I brushed it out, teased it very high and wild all over her head—it was in the days of the Bubble. Then I put down the brush and said very seriously, 'Thank you very much. I hope you enjoy your hair.'" Calmly leaving the booth, he smiled his way to the lunchroom to hide.

"Suddenly there was a shriek: 'He's not *serious*?' At which point I went back, finished combing her hair, and we had a good laugh," Kenneth recalled.

Another historic figure in his inner sphere was a colleague. Lesley Frowick, niece of American fashion designer Halston, shared, "I can confirm that Halston worked with Kenneth at Lilly Daché in 1957, and they remained friendly after he went to work at Bergdorf Goodman in 1958. Halston always sent his clients and family to the best hairdressers of the time—Kenneth was the first choice."

He charged $15 for a haircut, and he would instruct an assistant how to style each individual client. "As director of the salon, I only cut hair. The sets and other work were done by other people. It started as a way to cope with large numbers of clients, to keep my hand in, to have some relationship with each client. And it was the beginning of what's going on in hairdressing today—it started the upgrading of the haircut as the basis of a hairstyle," Kenneth said.

Although his day started before 9 a.m. and ended sometime after 9 p.m., albeit exhausted after a long day, Kenneth loved his job. Responsible for managing the salon, he did less editorial work than he had at Rubinstein's, missing it a little.

"I don't think I started anything, ever," Kenneth said. "All I did was start the day—every day—with the motto that 'If you are going to do something, do it well.'"

A moment in Kenneth's chair could go as such:

Lucille Ball, who famously called Kenneth "God," would also become a friend.

Mr. Kenneth

A special citation is in order for Mr. Kenneth of Lilly Daché, who generously contributed his time and his talent to GLAMOUR's 1961 College Fashion Show.

A possible insight into Mr. Kenneth is his favorite quotation from E. M. Forster's *Two Cheers for Democracy:*
"I believe in aristocracy—if that is the right word, and if a democrat may use it . . .
an aristocracy of the sensitive, the considerate and the plucky.
Its members are to be found in all nations and classes, and all through the ages, and there is
a secret understanding between them when they meet . . .
They represent the true human tradition, the one permanent victory of our queer race over cruelty and chaos.
Thousands of them perish in obscurity, a few are great names.
They are sensitive for others as well as for themselves, they are considerate without being fussy,
their pluck is not swankiness but the power to endure, and they can take a joke."

Italian actor Walter Chiari with model Monique Chevalier for *Vogue* in 1962. Kenneth believed that beautiful hair was the ultimate luxury.

Asked by a client, "How was your trip?"

"Around the world? Very wild. All those airplanes. Waiting to get into the palaces."

Kenneth methodically, again, cuts hair, pinning up, taking a few hairs at a time, getting the line straight. Another of the young men comes by, and Kenneth speaks to him:

"Did you get to the theater on time?"

"Yes, just barely. I showed her one of your hairdos— the one in GLAMOUR."

"With the hair coming into the eye?" says Kenneth. "The funny picture?"

"Yes. She thought you'd be insulted because she laughed."

Over the tenure of his time at Lilly Daché's salon, Kenneth liberated hair and ended the desire for hats. Between curating Jacqueline Kennedy's hair and creating her highly visible bouffant and the invention of hot rollers providing volume, hair became the hottest trend.

When she ascended to the White House, Kenneth followed. Gaining the unofficial title of "Secretary of Grooming," he was in charge of preparing her hair for major social events, including her husband's inauguration.

Finding it increasingly difficult to commute back and forth from Washington, DC, Kenneth solicited a local hairdresser to train and teach his hair techniques for her daily functions.

Newly elected president John F. Kennedy exchanges a few words with Vice President Lyndon B. Johnson at the Inaugural Ball at the Mayflower Hotel. Kenneth had changed Jacqueline's hairstyle to an evening look sans her signature pillbox hat.

"When he found out that he occasionally might have to be at the White House at 7:30 a.m., he didn't want the job. He turned it down. I was amazed—I would have been there at 3 a.m. if necessary," Kenneth said. "Maybe I was terribly naive, but it was always a tremendous thrill for me to go through the White House gates."

Gloria Vanderbilt visited him, deciding it was time to cut off her waist-length hair. "Sitting in the chair as he stood in back of me, I was somewhat hesitant—was I really certain that I really wanted to cut the hair I had worked so long to grow?" she remembered. "But as we conferred, there was no hesitation. Something about him I trust immediately. He was very low key, in no way aggressive, yet at the same time he had great authority. I knew that he sensed exactly what I was looking for and that he was the person to do it. I remember walking out onto the street that spring day with hair short—cut and styled by Kenneth—feeling happy, liberated, and free."

Jacqueline Kennedy on her husband's inauguration day on January 20, 1961.

Whether she was hosting a formal dinner or preparing for an appearance, Jacqueline Kennedy always called for Kenneth. Here, he landed in Washington, DC, on his way to the White House.

First Lady Jacqueline Kennedy with Prince Moulay Abdallah, brother of King Hassan II of Morocco.

Kenneth sitting on a sofa at the White House waiting for Jacqueline.

In 1963, the National Gallery of Art in Washington, DC, hosted the historic Mona Lisa in a temporary exhibition. Jacqueline Kennedy inaugurated the event with the minister of state for cultural affairs of France, André Malraux.

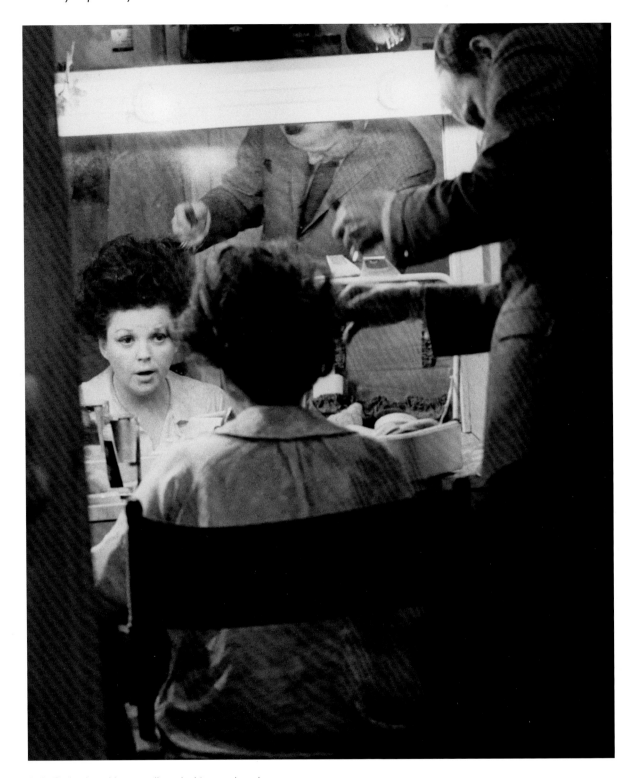

Judy Garland would eventually make history when she won a
Grammy Award for her live-recordings LP *Judy at Carnegie
Hall*—the first woman to do so. Kenneth prepared her hair
backstage for the performance, which was dubbed "the greatest
night in show business history."

Just like the fashion industry released a collection every season, Kenneth had done the same with hairstyles. Here, a press release photograph from the 1970s, modeled by Janice Dickinson in the earlier stages of her successful career.

Another casualty of the film industry's beauty department, Marilyn Monroe experienced her own traumatic experience similar to Kay Kendall's. In New York City after having filmed *Some Like It Hot*, Marilyn was steered to Kenneth by designer Norman Norell after crying that her hair was burned and badly damaged from the harsh bleaching.

"He [Norman Norell] gave her my name, and she called me from his showroom," Kenneth recalled. "Her secretary called me and asked me to come over to her apartment with my equipment. Of course, I was very excited by the whole idea. I took my bag of rollers and clips and I went. I waited very nervously in a white-and-beige foyer for about a half hour until Marilyn came in, in a white terry cloth robe and a big towel around her wet hair, just as nervous as I was. I was staggered by how beautiful she was just that way, with no makeup or hairdo.

"I blunted the ends of her hair and gave it a bias setting to try to overcome some of her strong wave pattern, making it look almost straight but turned up at the ends all the way around. She put on her makeup—it took her about an hour to do it, and then [she] wiped most of it off for a marvelous subtle effect—and then

the nude-color beaded chiffon dress that looked almost glued on her. She looked terrific. She was extremely shy and unsure of herself through this whole meeting. But I remember when she walked out later into a roomful of strangers, she suddenly became another woman, the woman we all saw in her pictures.

"I made her hair softer, smoother, and straighter. From then on, whenever she was in New York, she came to me at Daché or I went to her apartment at 444 East 57th Street. It took me about a year, but we got it to be very beautiful." He continued, "And she became my favorite steady client. She had wonderful hair; she had wonderful everything. She was one of the greatest people I've ever known."

In 1961, Marilyn asked Kenneth to prepare her for her release from the Columbia-Presbyterian Hospital.

"Arthur Miller declined to come, so Joe DiMaggio got her out instead," Kenneth recalled. "Marilyn was very vulnerable—the kindest, sweetest, most generous person I've ever known, period. And I don't mean generous with gifts. I mean generosity of spirit. That's why she was slapped down all the time, always getting hurt. Anyway, I went to help her make her exit from the hospital. She simply told me, 'I want to look good.'"

"When she came outside, I was absolutely staggered by the way her fans behaved. It was as if they owned her—as if she belonged to them. But Marilyn had that ability to make her movie audiences believe she would leap out of the screen and sit on their laps."

Heiress Gloria Vanderbilt and Kenneth shared a close friendship, a bond that lasted a lifetime. Having been captured by every major photographer, she always requested Kenneth to style her hair, notably in this iconic photo shoot with Richard Avedon in 1960.

Some Like It Hot Premiere | Chicago

In March 1959, Marilyn Monroe asked Kenneth to accompany her to Chicago for the premiere of *Some Like It Hot* at the United Artists Theatre.

"I went with her to prepare her for her stage appearance, of which she was terrified. I combed her hair out on the plane before we landed to confront a pushing, shoving, grabbing mob scene at the airport," Kenneth recalled.

"Marilyn didn't care much about clothes or jewelry," he continued. "Before we left, she went to Jax on 57th Street and 5th Avenue and bought three silk shifts—one in white, one in black, and one in tan. She borrowed a beige mink from Maximilian and took along two strings of pearls. When we got to the Ambassador East Hotel in Chicago, a movie PR guy spilled his glass of champagne down Marilyn's front. She was wearing the tan dress—and you could see everything, like she was in a wet T-shirt. She was going to throw the mink coat over the stains for the press conference, but I told her that if she wasn't changing her dress, she should at least put on some underwear. She said she wouldn't do that because underwear made lines."

Kenneth had made his way to the hotel drugstore and purchased all the ingredients needed for hair bleaching. He instructed her, "Now go in the bathroom and bleach the Y."

Once Marilyn was ready to confront the public, the night continued. It seemed like wherever she went, the chaos followed. "We piled into a car and headed for the theater—Marilyn, a publicity man, and myself. When we approached the theater, the car was suddenly surrounded by thousands of screaming people trying to get near her. They climbed on the car, trying to get in, to get a look at her, to touch her. I locked the doors as the mob started to rock the car back and forth, side to side. Marilyn was near hysterics, and we were all terrified. We inched our way forward and finally got to the theater entrance in a state of near collapse."

"I had thought, 'You'd have to be mad to want that kind of attention.' When the photographers crowded around after her appearance, Marilyn insisted that I be in the pictures too. Those pictures of Marilyn Monroe and Kenneth Battelle, formerly of Syracuse, were printed all over the world."

Touring the country to premiere and promote her film *Some Like It Hot*, Marilyn Monroe lands in Chicago at Midway Airport on March 17, 1959.

ROYALTY AROUND THE WORLD

In the sweltering heat of August 1961, Kenneth embarked on a voyage with Karlys Daly Brown, editor of *Glamour*, and Milton Greene, fashion photographer.

Traversing Africa, Asia, and the Middle East, they set out to photograph royals in various exotic countries for the magazine's Christmas issue.

"The idea with *Glamour* was to photograph royalty in these countries and bring a sense of Eastern magic to a Christmas issue. Unfortunately, whoever had been in charge with setting up the arrangements had

goofed, and everywhere we went, we were a complete surprise to the palace," Kenneth remembered.

Arriving in Morocco, the team's first stop was to photograph the sister of King Hassan. Since appropriate plans hadn't been confirmed and the palace in Rabat hadn't been notified that they'd be arriving, the team waited for two days after calling and explaining their intention. Finally an invitation was extended—the palace sent a car to collect them at the hotel past sunset.

Upon arriving at their destination, they received permission from the guards to pass through the daunting gates, then trek through a courtyard and an entrance to finally wait in a reception room. Within seconds, without any warning, the resilient lights went out all across the palace.

After what seemed like an eternity, someone emerged with a candle to escort them through the blackened corridors and a labyrinth of rooms. Reaching a grand room dimly lit by candles, they were introduced to the princess, who consented to having her photograph taken after they explained the reason for their visit.

"We chose a beautiful ceremonial robe with an enormous jeweled belt for her to wear," Kenneth reminisced. "Unfortunately, when we finally saw the princess in the light, we discovered that like many women in Morocco, she hennaed her hair. Because she hadn't expected us, she hadn't had her henna pack in quite some time. About two inches of her own dark hair showed; the rest was red." The pictures were taken, but they were never used for the December issue.

Her Royal Highness Princess Muna Al-Hussein of Jordan

Next on the itinerary was Amman, Jordan, to photograph King Hussein's new wife, Muna, but the trio was unannounced once again. By the next day, almost mirroring their prior stop, they were requested to appear at the palace and explain their mission. Once they passed the guards' inspection, this time they were accompanied to the king's quarters. He greeted them, curiously listened to their request, and then introduced them to his wife before departing.

"I trimmed her hair and set it. When it was dry, she went to her closet and picked out a pale-blue-green dress to wear. We all went out on the terrace, which overlooked the entire city. Below us were a row of guards with machine guns," said Kenneth.

Morocco.

A spot was chosen for her to stand where the city sprawled behind her. The intense heat of summer had been baking everything within its reach.

"I went over to her to pin her hair on the side because it was blowing in the breeze, and as I did it, she slumped to the floor. She had fainted! I nearly fainted too," Kenneth said.

Instinctively, they rushed to grab the collapsed queen off the floor. Suddenly Kenneth shouted for everyone to back away and not touch her, fearing that the machine guns downstairs would storm the terrace. Fortunately, the compassionate queen allowed them to return the following day to snap the perfect photograph where the pair "spent a wonderful time talking about fashion and makeup."

Pushing eastward, he also made an appearance in the palaces of Iran, India, and Thailand. Everywhere his scissors and brushes worked, Kenneth from New York City left a touch of elegance.

Jordan.

Her Majesty Empress Farah Pahlavi of Iran

Mesmerized by the empress's beauty, the Iranian government placed her photograph from the photo shoot in every embassy.

Iran.

Her Highness Begum Saleha Sultan of Bhopal

"Testing the memories of seniors is futile; however, seeing the clear and lovely camerawork, reflections come alive. Kenneth was truly a famous hairdresser. The shape of the hairstyle would change imperceptibly until it matched the mood and personality of his client. It's a beautiful memory from so many years ago.

"It was a very exciting experience for me, age twenty, pregnant with my son, when I was requested to do a photo shoot for *Glamour* magazine. I remember the pictures taken at the top floor of the Ashoka Hotel (today named the Ashok) in Delhi. My friend arranged everything, so I walked into the photo shoot with my aide without knowing what was happening. I was so delighted with my new look, and it was gratifying that it subjected my husband to a heart condition later on. I looked very glamorous, much more than usual. I didn't go to hairdressers at that age because I was very young, so I didn't know much about them or makeup, but I was made very beautiful. They took my picture multiple times, and I enjoyed every minute."

India.

Her Royal Highness Princess Jeet Nabha Khemka of India

"Kenneth was very charming. The first time I met him was when he came to India, and after that, every time I went to New York I used to go to him."

India.

Her Majesty Queen Sirikit of Thailand

Kenneth received special treatment upon arriving in Thailand. He was granted permission to style the queen's hair after Her Majesty Queen Sirikit temporarily suspended the law forbidding anyone to stand above or over her.

Thailand.

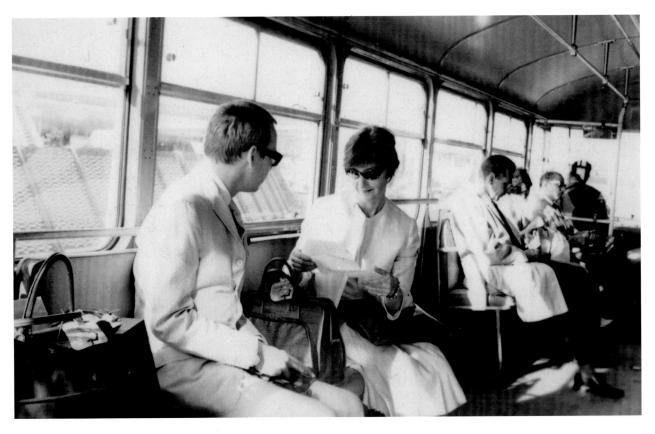

A Coty Award to the One & Only Hairdresser

During World War II, the demand for fabrics tremendously increased as the war effort was to be supported around the world. The military needed an abundance of cotton, wool, and nylon; Japanese silk was banned due to soured foreign relations. Governments placed restrictions on the use of fabrics, and clothing became scarce. Suddenly clothes had become rationed, and Paris, which had been at the epicenter of fashion, had lost its momentum. In 1942, seeing it as an opportunity instead of a challenge, global beauty company Coty debuted the Coty American Fashion Critics' Awards.

The bronze award trophy, created by famed American sculptor Malvina Hoffman, was dubbed *Winnie*. Publicly, a Winnie was awarded to fashion designers who excelled in design, but it was also intended to stimulate competition within the industry in the United States. With the European collections slowing down to a trickle, "the American Look" across the Atlantic Ocean had become highly coveted.

Kenneth explained: "The Coty Award was dreamed up by Eleanor Lambert as a promotional idea for Coty perfume and makeup." Nonetheless, it

THE 19th ANNUAL
COTY
AMERICAN
FASHION
CRITICS'
AWARD

In collaboration with the Costume Institute, Metropolitan Museum of Art

GRACE RAINEY ROGERS AUDITORIUM
METROPOLITAN MUSEUM OF ART
SEPTEMBER 28, 1961

The official program for the award ceremony on September 28, 1961.

FOREWORD

Since it was founded in 1943, the Coty American Fashion Critics' Award has been the fashion world's most coveted honor. Through the years, the Award trophy known as Winnie, a bronze sculptured figure by Malvina Hoffman, has gone to many kinds of superlatives in American fashion. It has gone to creativity, to integrity, to high standards of workmanship and even to the editing instinct when it amounts to genius. Each Fall the presentation ceremony, before an important audience, has provided an impressive setting for the mushrooming power and importance of American fashion.

The jury, composed of over 80 fashion editors, experienced in different phases of the fashion world, votes with complete sincerity and conviction. It tries to recognize fresh talent when it appears. It also seeks to crystalize appreciation for mature designers and to give delayed recognition to their impact through the years.

The question most asked—what makes a designer award material in the eyes of the American Fashion Critics? He must have the creative imagination and skill to turn fluid fabrics into clothes of contemporary beauty and use. But if he is to add so much as a paragraph to fashion history, he must also have humor, a complete understanding of his time and—the unique American must—the capacity to synchronize his self expression to the fast beat of industrial productivity.

This year, the American Fashion Critics add a new name to their Hall of Fame—the ultimate award they can bestow. Enrollment in the Hall of Fame signifies three awards for superlatives in any phase of fashion. To the present Hall of Fame roster—Norman Norell, James Galanos, Pauline Trigere and the late Claire McCardell—the jury now adds the name of Ben Zuckerman. The award recognizes the unflagging spirit, vitality and manufacturing perfection of his coat and suit collections.

Two young men receive Winnies for the first time. A New York designer, Bill Blass and west coast designer, Gustave Tassell, are both commended for raising the standards of American fashion imagination and elegance.

Special awards go to a designer who has already won a Winnie and, for the first time, to a hair stylist. The designer, Bonnie Cashin, is American to her fingertips, so American that her country clothes of tweed and leather have greatly influenced European fashions. In an era that believes in the importance of hair-do's, stylist Kenneth Battelle is not only at the top of his profession in this country but is recognized throughout the world.

EUGENIA SHEPPARD
Women's Feature Editor, New York Herald Tribune
Member CAFCA jury

FASHION SHOWING 1961

COTY AMERICAN FASHION CRITICS' AWARD / METROPOLITAN MUSEUM OF ART, SEPTEMBER 28, 1961

KENNETH of LILLY DACHE
Highlights of his hair designs...
Forecast of Coiffure Fashions...

BILL BLASS of MAURICE RENTNER LTD.
Designs from his Fall, Winter and
Resort 1961-62 Collections...

BONNIE CASHIN
Designs in leather and fabrics
for Philip Sills

COTY HALL OF FAME
NORMAN NORELL—1944
PAULINE TRIGERE—1959
JAMES GALANOS—1959

BEN ZUCKERMAN—1961
Highlights of his current collection

GUSTAVE TASSELL
Designs from his Fall, Winter and
Resort 1961-62 Collections...

BONNIE CASHIN

To classify Bonnie Cashin as a sportswear designer is a misnomer as she creates clothes for every occasion of modern living—from elegant garments to wear at home, on country weekends, at ski resorts, or deep-country roughing it, to trans-world jet liners and ocean transports, to bicycling and mountain climbing. Her scope is international yet her fashions are uniquely American, informal yet sophisticated.

Miss Cashin has never been to Tibet but her 1961 resort and travel collection, presented in the leather-tangy, aromatic showrooms of Philip Sills, her manufacturer, showed the first high-style Llamasary modes, wearable anywhere in the world.

Since the day she left San Francisco for New York to try her design-wings, Miss Cashin has always taken an independent route to success. Her first efforts were clothes for the ballet and theatre, plus a fling at sportswear. This brought her to the attention of Hollywood who dangled a 6-year contract before her—so she went west. During that time she designed clothes, both period and modern, for 60 major films, including the beautifully costumed "Anna and the King of Siam" and the unforgettable "Laura."

Inventive (her father was an inventor, her mother a dressmaker), her ponchos double as lap robes . . . her Cashin-carry leather bags accessorize a costume as well as perform their usual function. Rainwear, knitwear and leather industries are glad to stand up and cheer, she being the first to design light and white raincoats, for taking the hunchiness out of knitwear. As for leather—she has placed it on a high fashion level and endowed it with an easy, relaxed style.

Manufacturer Philip Sills has this to say, "Miss Cashin is a generative designer. Though we present her fashions each season we know they are seasonless. Each of her designs recreates itself in a related way because almost any Cashin garment goes well with almost any other Cashin garment." This accounts for their globe-trotting ability to circuit anywhere at any time of year, leaving a longing memory in other countries for their zestful, free-world look, so young, so at ease, and yet forever on the go-go-go.

KENNETH of LILLY DACHE

Kenneth Battelle, better known as Kenneth of Lilly Dache, has turned more heads toward fashion consciousness than any hair stylist of recent times. His present link with the most celebrated, most photographed and, by popular acclaim, the loveliest First Coiffure in the world is the apex of a career solidly based on training and technical skill as well as a creative eye for the outline of a head in proportion to the current points and counterpoints of fashion silhouettes.

Any Monday morning finds under the dryer in the Lilly Dache salon at least ten of the models whose faces and figures reflected by the interpretative lens of such camera greats as Richard Avedon, Milton Greene and Irving Penn, train the eye to the new proportions and subtle exaggerations which eventually form the look of the season.

Kenneth Battelle was born in Syracuse, New York where his father was in the retail and wholesale shoe business. He was educated at the University of Syracuse, majoring in the fine arts. The eldest of five children, he dropped out of college so that his earnings could help educate his sisters. His interest in portrait sculpture found transference in designing coiffures, and he found a job at a local hairdresser before coming to New York to work and study at the same time.

During the second World War he served with the United States Navy in, to him, the extremely dull assignment of recruiting. Though he wanted to be in the middle of things, he was sent on nation-wide recruiting tours, playing the piano and singing rousing songs to urge other young men to join the service. "Much as I hated it," he says now, "I must admit I learned a great deal about America and human nature."

Kenneth, a tall, slender blonde young man with an imperturbable calm gives the impression of being as typical a New Yorker as can be found, probably because he loves New York and all that goes on in it. He is an avid first nighter, reads the columns, and lives alone in a skyscraper apartment with a much-indulged taupe poodle.

Kenneth's award today—faded by time and damaged by smoke from the salon's fire.

annually became the most prestigious award within the industry, often being compared to the Oscars of the fashion world.

On the suggestion of Diana Vreeland, and not fully agreeable to the fashion industry, in 1961 Kenneth was awarded. He became the first and only hairdresser in the history of the Coty Awards. "It was quite exciting as it had not been given to a hair person before. It's always nice to be a first." Unlike the designers, who received a Winnie sculpture, Kenneth's was a special plaque.

Ceremony day, September 28, was held at the Grace Rainey Rogers Auditorium at the Metropolitan Museum of Art in collaboration with the Costume Institute. That evening, Kenneth was in royal company of some of the industry's greatest pioneers: Bill Blass (first American couture fashion designer to start a menswear collection), Bonnie

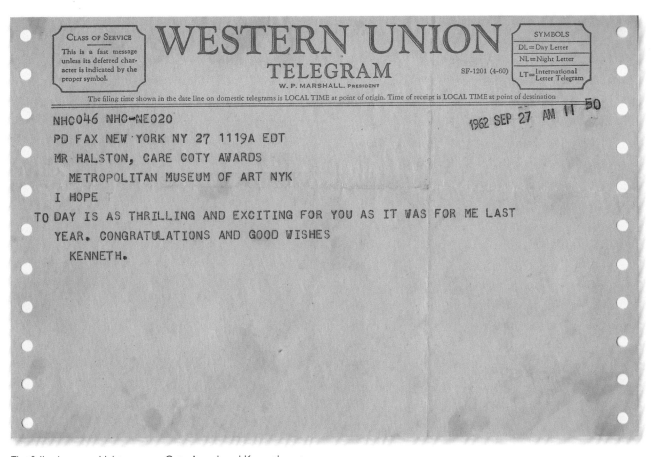

CLASS OF SERVICE

This is a fast message unless its deferred character is indicated by the proper symbol.

W. P. MARSHALL, PRESIDENT

SF-1201 (4-60)

SYMBOLS
DL=Day Letter
NL=Night Letter
LT=International Letter Telegram

The filing time shown in the date line on domestic telegrams is LOCAL TIME at point of origin. Time of receipt is LOCAL TIME at point of destination

NHC046 NHC-NE020

1962 SEP 27 AM 11 50

PD FAX NEW YORK NY 27 1119A EDT

MR HALSTON, CARE COTY AWARDS

METROPOLITAN MUSEUM OF ART NYK

I HOPE T

TO DAY IS AS THRILLING AND EXCITING FOR YOU AS IT WAS FOR ME LAST

YEAR. CONGRATULATIONS AND GOOD WISHES

KENNETH.

The following year, Halston won a Coty Award, and Kenneth sent him a congratulatory telegram.

Cashin (a trailblazer in American sportswear), Gustave Tassell (one of America's hottest new designers), and Ben Zuckerman ("the Master Tailor of Seventh Avenue").

Rehearsals had been held earlier that day, but Kenneth had found it to be an unpleasant experience. None of the other winners exchanged many words with him, and there was an air of slight discontent; someone who wasn't part of 7th Avenue had been awarded. Eleanor Lambert, who was in command of the event, would yell from the audience, telling the finalists where to move around onstage, particularly Kenneth. Afterward, surrounded by a few of his closest friends while holding his plaque, Kenneth, who was only thirty-four years old, had just made history once again.

Happy Birthday, Mr. President

On the evening of May 19, 1962, Kenneth arrived at 444 East 57th Street to visit Marilyn Monroe at her apartment. Having started as a client, she eventually became "a really good friend." The friendship had reached a level of understanding where there was no need to explain to one another. When she was in New York City, the two spent time together. He would provide her with a wig, and the pair would go shopping or have lunch and no one would recognize her.

That particular night, her neighborhood of Sutton Place was quiet, although hours later, chaos would engulf New York City. Marilyn was to sing "Happy Birthday" to President John F. Kennedy at Madison Square Garden for a Democratic Party fundraising gala (although the president would not celebrate his forty-fifth birthday until ten days later, on May 29). It was to be an evening of celebrity performances and tributes: songstresses Ella Fitzgerald and Peggy Lee, comedian Jack Benny, crooner Harry Belafonte, and opera diva Maria Callas were featured on the bill. Marilyn was determined to ensure that her appearance was unparalleled, and unforgettable.

She bedazzled the audience in a clinging Jean Louis gown of nude-colored, lightweight mesh fabric, emblazoned by thousands of rhinestones—so minimal, yet so resilient. A design based off a sketch by Bob Mackie and originally created for Marlene Dietrich to wear during her concert shows, the dress had caught Marilyn's attention. Marlene, who explained to Monroe that the playfulness of the design lay in its strategically placed rhinestones, sent Marilyn to Jean Louis to have one custom made especially for the birthday performance.

Kenneth had carefully combed and shaped her platinum tresses, keeping them straight and simple while focusing all the attention on a dramatic cascading swoop on the right side of her face. Once her hair was styled, her makeup pale and shimmery, her dress

and jewels radiant, Marilyn stepped from her car in front of Madison Square Garden—at the time it had been on 8th Avenue between 49th Street and 50th Street—to a frenzy of fans and paparazzi.

"Marilyn did not want me backstage with her," Kenneth recalled. "She said she was fearful of publicity. I don't know what she had in mind, but since I was doing both Marilyn and Mrs. Kennedy at the same time, I imagine it was about that."

First Lady Jacqueline Kennedy did not attend the event that evening, and all eyes were on Marilyn. "She looked gorgeous. Funnily enough, if you see pictures of her that night when she's getting into her car at her apartment and arriving at Madison Square Garden, that's my hairdo. There was a union hairdresser there who recombed and teased her hair more. I preferred it beforehand, but when you're at a huge place like Madison Square Garden, you need huge hair."

Marilyn had strategized. She knew exactly what she was doing, and had rehearsed her performance well beforehand. Before stepping out in front of the crowd at the auditorium, she ran around backstage to make herself slightly breathless. In her signature style of being beyond tardy, Marilyn finally appeared to belt out her sultry, seductive rendition of "Happy Birthday."

Renowned American jazz artist Hank Jones accompanied her on the piano, and she added lyrics from the classic song "Thanks for the Memory," words she specifically aimed at the president. The song finished with a jubilant Marilyn shouting, "Everybody, Happy Birthday!," followed by a staggering birthday cake carried by two men.

Moments later onstage, the president thanked all of the night's performers, sarcastically adding a special nod to Marilyn: "I can now retire from politics after having had 'Happy Birthday' sung to me in such a sweet, wholesome way." The next morning, newspapers were filled with photographs of Marilyn serenading Kennedy in her knockout dress and teased tresses a la Kenneth—an immeasurable scandal. It would be one of her last major public appearances.

THE LAST SITTING WITH MARILYN MONROE

In June 1962, weeks after Marilyn's presidential birthday sensation, Kenneth flew to Los Angeles to unite with her and fashion photographer Bert Stern for a photo shoot that *Vogue* had commissioned. Accompanying him on the trip was close confidante and *Vogue* fashion editor Babs Simpson. She had been responsible for selecting the wardrobe, bringing fur coats and designer dresses in tow.

"Kenneth was so famous that in the Los Angeles airport, people stopped him for autographs," Babs amusedly recalled.

Having been asked once in an interview what was his favorite editorial sitting, Kenneth's response had been simple: "Any with Babs Simpson as editor."

Bert Stern had surmised that the magazine sent her, whom he called "the needlepoint editor," since she had become known for keeping herself busy by sewing in the corner during downtime, because she would let him "be the most creative and at the same time keep the most control." *Vogue* wanted the clothes to remain on Marilyn.

The sitting, which was staged for several days at a partially concealed bungalow at the Bel-Air Hotel, number 96 to be exact, would historically become dubbed "the Last Sitting." Once most of the furniture was cleared from the bedroom, the makeshift studio then filled with the latest fashion, intoxicating sexual energy, and abundant bottles of 1953 Dom Pérignon—Marilyn's favorite.

More than 2,000 photographs were taken for the project. As Babs alternated dresses on Marilyn, a frustrated Bert believed that the blonde goddess's beauty was most admired with less clothing covering her voluptuous body. Kenneth rotated wigs and hairpieces, keeping up with the wardrobe's rhythm.

"As she was posing for the last shot—lying on the floor with her hair spread out all around—I had to run for the airport to catch my plane. She asked me to kiss her goodbye," Kenneth recalled. "I have always wished

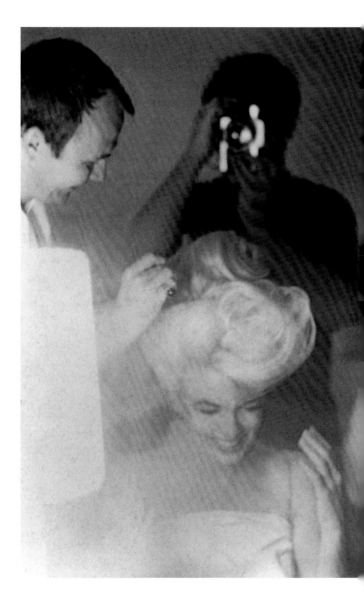

I'd recognized the depth of her loneliness—perhaps I could've been a better friend if I had."

This was the final time that Kenneth would style Marilyn's hair; six weeks later she made the front page of the *Los Angeles Times* with the headline "Marilyn Monroe Found Dead."

The House of Kenneth at 19 East 54th Street

For years, Kenneth had envisioned owning his own salon, a House of Beauty, inspired by the glamour of Hollywood movies he had indulged in as a child. His, however, was far from the expected. It was a work of art constructed of chiffon drapes, hundreds of doorways with mysteries behind each one, walls splashed with many colors, different floors with different services—a total unconventional experience.

"I was a child of the '30s," Kenneth once stated, "and in the movies of the '30s, beauty salons were great, extraordinary places where you saw people running through in all kinds of go-to-the-beauty-parlor costumes with dogs on leashes and all kinds of madness, and that was my idea of a house of beauty."

"It took six months for him to be satisfied to find a place where he wanted his salon, because in his head, it wasn't a salon like everyone else had. In his head, it was an invention of a dream," remembered Amy Greene, wife of fashion photographer Milton Greene.

He wanted a majestic palace of pampering, something that would break the predictable standard that had taken hold in beauty parlors across the country. Although he had multiple clients offering to assist in bringing his project to fruition, Kenneth wanted to make sure it was done right. To make his dream a reality, he waited for the most compatible investor.

"My husband, Milton, and Kenneth were very, very close," Amy Greene explained. "And when this salon idea was in the air, Kenneth said, 'We need a lot of money.' I remember watching them, endlessly writing on legal pads of paper—$50,000; $75,000; scratched out and then $100,000, and so on. Milton had said, 'Well, I don't think you want to ask your clients.' Mrs. Mellon could've easily written a check, but that's not the way Kenneth thought."

Kenneth recalled, "Wealthy clients wanted to back me in business, but it didn't seem the right thing to do. One very stimulating man, who was very inspiring and gave me confidence, believed in my vision as much as I, gave me the strength and the desire to go ahead. But when he suggested that we make 'First Lady Perfume,' I thought it was in very bad taste. Because of a detail like that, I dropped the whole thing."

Charles Revson, founder of Revlon and an ever-ingenious entrepreneur, wanted more than anything to be a part of Kenneth's world. He was going to give Kenneth anything: "Write your own check and I'll sign it." Charles wanted class; he wanted what drove the ladies wild. He called Kenneth and said, "Go look at this salon on 5th Avenue, it's next to Harry Winston." Convinced to give it a chance, Kenneth, Milton Greene, and his wife, Amy, walked in only to discover a shrine to the color black—black marble floors and black marble walls, barely visible in the low lighting. There was a discreet pool with fish swimming, which proved to be a hazard. After touring the entire location, once outside on the sidewalk Kenneth said, "If the man gave me a bag with a million dollars, I could not do this. It's out of the question. I cannot work with this man." Very disappointed at Kenneth's response, Charles had Milton explain: "It's all black for Christ's sake. That's not his style."

"Well, I'll get rid of the black. Whatever he wants." The deal never happened.

In 1962, his search proved successful as he financially partnered up with Milton Greene and the Glemby Company, a family-owned beauty company of salons and products. Kenneth had 40 percent, Glemby 50 percent, and Milton 10 percent; Kenneth bought out Milton years later.

The professional marriage was the foundation to Kenneth's aspirations—a three-tier plan to open a top salon under the Kenneth name, create a line of beauty products to be sold nationally, and bring Glemby the knowledge and expertise of the Kenneth organization. It enabled him to take out an extraordinary fifty-year lease at a perfectly preserved Renaissance Revival townhouse at 19 East 54th Street, built in 1900.

The Kenneth Salon at 19 East 54th Street in New York City.

Prior to 1920, the austere granite Italian palazzo was home to Minnie Young, a socialite whose elite neighbors included John D. Rockefeller, banker Philip Lehman, and W. E. D. Stokes, founding father of the Upper West Side. When the neighborhood slowly morphed from residential to commercial and Mrs. Young followed her affluent contemporaries uptown,

The inside of the Italian palazzo before its transformation into a salon. Kenneth would enlist the assistance of famed interior decorator Billy Baldwin to make his vision come to life.

her home was converted into a store—show windows were installed at ground level, and the iron fence was removed. It changed ownership and purpose several times before Kenneth stepped in. Designed by Hiss & Weekes, the same architectural firm responsible for the Peninsula Hotel in New York City, the townhouse was 17,000 square feet of elegance: marble Corinthian columns, elaborate cornices, a handsome wood-paneled staircase, opulent floors, and a coffered-dome ceiling.

"I wanted to keep the sense of a private home and to have a luxurious comfort that would also be practical. I had seen the Brighton Pavilion in England not long before, and I loved the sheer mad fantasy, the sense of humor and luxury of it. That was the effect I wanted in my salon," Kenneth said.

To concretize his mental images of what the space should look like, Kenneth employed renowned American interior designer Billy Baldwin to transform the five-story structure.

"I asked Billy Baldwin to do the decorating," remembered Kenneth, "and it worked out just the way I wanted it to."

At first, Billy had been either slightly skeptical or in utter shock. Kenneth knew exactly what he wanted and how he wanted it and what needed to be. It was the first time the two gentlemen had met. Although Kenneth and he shared similar clients—Bunny Mellon, Babe Paley, and Diana Vreeland—Billy, who had been the era's most coveted interior designer, had never accepted commercial projects. This one would be a departure from his usual modus operandi; he would be designing for a million women and not for one, knowing it would be monumental in interior design.

As the pair toured the townhouse, Billy asked, "How do you see this place?"

"Amusing. Like the Brighton Pavilion—an extravagant folly built by a king out of his mind. I want it to have a circus quality—all red, yellow, and white with tents. . . . My favorite colors are red and yellow. I want a Chinese lamp on every newel post going up the stairs, and pattern on pattern everywhere," Kenneth had answered. The small-town boy from Syracuse had vastly evolved. Pointing to a wood-paneled wall that resembled something from a house designed by Frank Lloyd Wright, he continued, "I cannot bear oak as a color."

"I think I could probably do all of that."

Captivated by its decadent interiors and rich colors, Kenneth used the Royal Pavilion, also known as the Brighton Pavilion, as inspiration for 19 East 54th Street.

And so they did. The metamorphosis was a mélange of the wildest color palette, a burst of visual energy and excitement. Opulent, decadent, and exuberant.

"We used a lot of pattern on pattern, cotton-draped walls, wicker furniture, flowered carpeting, lacquer paint in brilliant colors," Kenneth remembered. "I avoided all the fake French dressing room décor that so many salons had, stayed away from the aqua, baby-blue, and gold angels, and that kind of thing. As a result, there was a wonderful sense of luxury and humor and permanence about the place."

Billy Baldwin once wrote about Kenneth's salon, describing the project: "Paisley on paisley splashed on. The material is cotton—yards and yards of it, used really on a mammoth scale. We swagged it, draped it, tented it, all of it richly colored—scarlet, blue, butter yellow—and filled and surrounded with layer upon layer of pattern. I thought it would be great fun for a woman to have her hair dried under a paisley tent, her fingertips manicured on a Porthault pillow, her hair curled by the light of a palm-tree lamp, as she sits in a lacquered bamboo chair."

After eight months of decorating, and armed with equipment of the latest innovation in the beauty world, Kenneth's fantasy palace opened on March 4, 1963,

The vestibule to the salon's second floor.

The tented drying room anchored by the Regency crystal chandelier.

The styling stations on the second floor.

Drapes were omnipresent in his salon—Kenneth believed in the utmost privacy for his clients.

with an inaugural celebration attended by his friends, staff, and upper-society clientele.

"My mother just loved Kenneth. When he quit, he put in a six-month notice!" laughed Suzanne Daché, daughter of Lilly Daché.

Social commentator Cleveland Amory dubbed the salon "archrevolutionary."

Kenneth stated that for the first time in the history of hair salons, "clients could be hidden away during the messiest processes, something unique in the world."

Glamour declared that there was "more joyous ornament and detail at Kenneth's than in an entire collection of Matisse paintings."

Kenneth's grand opening party was attended by his A-list clients, including Lauren Bacall.

Babe Paley toured Kenneth's sumptuous salon on the night of its grand opening.

Best friend and top model Missy Bancroft at Kenneth's celebration, seen with illustrious fashion reporter Eugenia Sheppard.

Although her sister, Jacqueline, did not attend, fashion icon Lee Radziwill made an appearance to celebrate Kenneth's newest business venture.

Grand opening night.

"We had some very funny reactions to it," Kenneth said of the feedback he received. "Some people said it looked like a Chinese restaurant. Others said it looked like a bordello. All of which pleased me, because nobody said it looked like a beauty salon," he smirked.

Ladies all across the country wanted to be a part of 19 East 54th Street. The waiting list to book an appointment was a few months long. It was an oasis of elegance, a sanctuary in the midst of the craziness of New York City. Upon arriving at the front of the townhouse, clients were greeted by artistic installations, fantasies created by prominent window decorator Gene Moore. Also the display director for Tiffany & Co.'s 5th Avenue windows, Gene would have people lined down the block to see what visions his mind conjured. He brought this same magic to the salon.

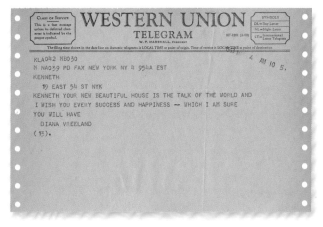

Diana Vreeland, editor in chief of *Vogue*.

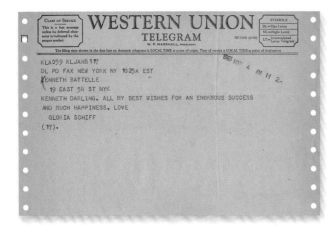

Gloria Schiff, socialite and editor of *Vogue*.

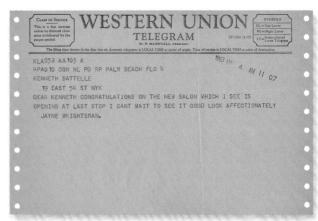

Jayne Wrightsman, philanthropist and fine-arts collector.

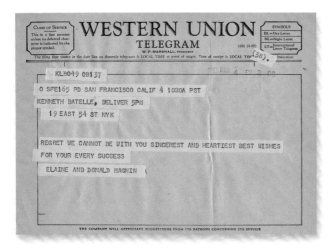

Elaine and Donald Magnin, part of the famed San Francisco department store family.

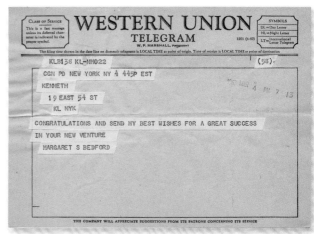

Margaret Bedford, oil heiress and duchess.

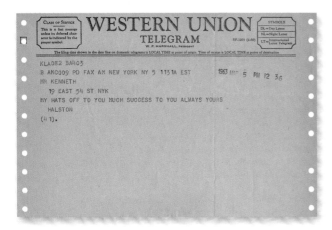

Halston, a leading American fashion designer.

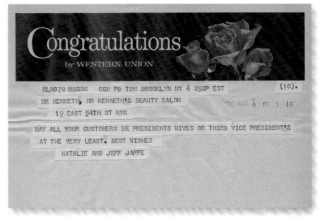

Natalie and Jeff Jaffe, family to the Tootsie Roll dynasty.

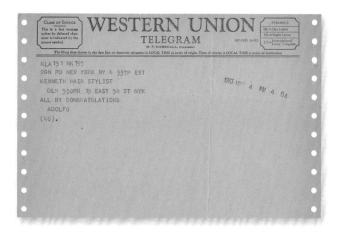

Adolfo, award-winning American fashion designer.

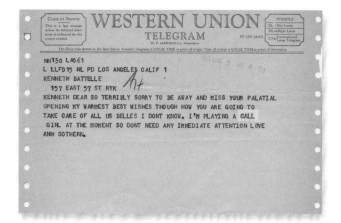

Ann Sothern, American actress whose career spanned almost six decades.

Renowned for his window displays at Tiffany & Co., Gene Moore brought his theatrical magic to the Kenneth Salon.

Kenneth had decided not to advertise beauty products in his windows.

"But rather to sell an idea . . . an inspiration. 'Real hair' windows get un-fresh too fast. In order to look good, they must be changed often. Our windows are seasonal and are changed about every three months," Kenneth explained.

Upon entering the massive wrought-iron fretwork doors, guests were greeted by the receptionist; to the left were paisley changing rooms, to the right a small boutique. (A decade later, the wig salon would be on the right and the boutique would be shifted to the left; the changing rooms were pushed to the back.) Walking toward the back and passing the

elevator, one would encounter a charming retro telephone booth. A hidden styling room also composed the ground floor, often used to prevent mistresses from encountering wives. Fur coats were hung in a special cold-storage closet.

Ascending the handsome staircase to the second floor, clients discovered a cavernous paisley-tented drying room anchored by a dazzling blue chandelier, as well as the combing and setting rooms invaded by bamboo and trellises. Potted palm trees added to the jungle aura, and oriental mirrors adorned with red-lacquer frames added a touch of exotic.

On the third floor were the rooms for tinting and shampooing, decorated with black patent-leather

chairs, white counters, and terra-cotta sinks, "as antiseptic as surgeries," *Vogue* observed in 1963.

If the bible of fashion compared his cleanliness to that of hospitals, one of his most loyal followers saw him as the doctor. "He's a surgeon when it comes to cutting hair," Susan Newhouse once exclaimed.

Kenneth's room, as if painted by Gustav Klimt with its golden, summery paisley print, was also located on the third floor, where his top stylists toiled, dressed in suits and ties. The sun-drenched fourth floor was devoted to physical fitness. There, clients indulged in darkened massage rooms, whirlpool baths, the hot sauna room made of redwood, waxing chambers, and a Pilates studio. Drapes were placed on every window, on every floor, to shut out the outside world; utmost privacy was mandatory.

"For a beauty salon, we're out on an awfully long limb," Kenneth admitted to the *New Yorker*'s Lillian Ross, the first client on opening day. She had once

come as a reporter and ended up being converted to a weekly client.

Former editor in chief of *Vogue* Grace Mirabella proclaimed, "Kenneth's salon wasn't your typical soupy, sugary vision of loveliness—nor was it sharp and tough. If you were doing decorating of any kind, elements of its design would definitely catch your eye."

No matter how elaborate the décor, the business was steered by Kenneth's philosophy of providing exquisite customer service. Preferring that his staff didn't greet their clients with kisses on the cheeks, he also asked that all the customers be addressed by their surnames. He never advertised his salon—customers came by word of mouth. A status symbol within the industry, working for Kenneth meant tremendous respect. He brought class to hairdressing.

A steward of society, he instructed stage actress Elizabeth Ashley on how to seductively remove a hair-piece while performing, cut and styled Carol Channing's

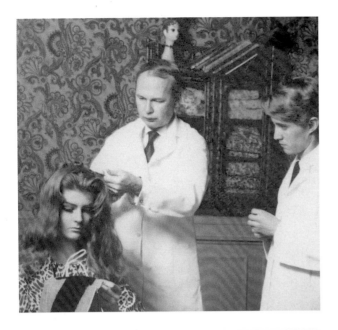

Lalla Nuzha of Morocco had shared with a newspaper that what appealed most to her about New York cultural life was her visit with Kenneth.

"I believe in coddle, coddle, coddle," Kenneth said. Clients were to be treated like royalty; comfort and relaxation were never to be forfeited. Maids served handcrafted gourmet sandwiches from William Poll on fancy printed trays; a black Mercedes-Benz station wagon was at their disposal to be used as a personal taxi, charioting clients to the salon or wherever was their next appointment; ladies were gifted a bottle of their nail lacquer color after a manicure; and the clients wore robes of printed cotton with a drawstring that Kenneth had designed. Mistresses and wives were to avoid running into one another at all times, which Kenneth ensured by instructing the staff to service each on different floors. Though, at times, keeping the two separated could be a challenge, he always made it happen.

Kenneth with good friend and top model Gillis MacGill in the sauna of the Kenneth Salon.

hair before she embarked on her theatrical tour of George Bernard Shaw's *The Millionairess*, and had Christina Onassis follow her stepmother Jacqueline Kennedy to his salon chair.

Famed postmodern architect Philip Johnson once confided that he was pressured to quickly finish constructing the AT&T Building at 550 Madison Avenue so that his friends could arrive unobstructed to the Kenneth Salon. Her Royal Highness Princess

Kenneth greatly disliked the idea of tipping, finding it to be corruptive and the hindering of a service from becoming a profession. He always kindly refused tips even after acknowledging the amount of money lost in the span of his career. No matter how much he forbade it, some ladies still insisted. When he first opened 19 East 54th Street, he tried to eradicate tipping by replacing it with a service charge as they did in Europe. However, the change proved to be futile, since the other hairdressers were dispirited about the idea, and no matter how much the salon tried, the ladies would still leave a tip. Small envelopes were provided at the front desk, where a client could leave whatever she wished in case she objected to handing money to the hairdresser or awkwardly stuffing it in their pockets.

Kenneth remembered when he first started at Rubinstein's: "I had no clue whatsoever about money in those days. I never paid the slightest attention to the fact that after your basic salary, your money came through commissions, which were 25 percent on each paying customer. The other hairdressers were all more street-smart moneywise than I was; they realized that every time they did a client gratis, they weren't going to take home a commission."

With the charm to define him as much as his perfectly tailored suits, and gray-blue eyes to captivate, Kenneth was a handsome gentleman. The ladies of Park Avenue swooned over him. Secretly, they vied for his companionship. Not only was he a locked vault with all of their secrets, Kenneth had them sit in his chair and desperately desire to make them the women who they were, or wished to be. He was an enigma who possessed an infectious sense of humor and a boyish smile to accommodate. With wit as sharp as his famous scissors, he always said that when he died, he wanted to be cremated and have his ashes thrown off the top of the Empire State Building—there were a few women in New York whose eye he wanted to get into. If he started a statement with "*Did you hear this one . . . ?*," it was well known that a joke was about to follow.

Although engaging, he was also stern. His business was governed with a level of expectation that neared perfection; he would tell his employees what he wanted and what he didn't prefer.

He had the same demeanor that Mrs. Kennedy had, as well as Mrs. Mellon. A generation that sent handwritten notes, they were of a traditional, well-brought-up American education in social conduct.

"Remember," described Lillian Ross, "you are dealing with an artist. An artist with scissors."

Kenneth became the first celebrity hairdresser, according to the *New York Times*. His fame had catapulted him to being a household name, and he was referenced as "Hairdresser to the Stars."

He wasn't one to be victim to his ego, learning very early in his career by watching others diminish their talent by their eccentric behavior. Kenneth attributed his longevity to his willingness to listen and be patient. Publicity was nothing but a mere form of marketing, a source of business. It wasn't meant to define someone; it was only supposed to push business forward. He received a fresh wave of new clients by his regulars who were noticed at a soiree or on the street.

"All the publicity in the world, no matter how many times your name is in the newspapers or pictures of your hairstyles are in magazines, really doesn't make you as well known as a happy client, a woman who looks at herself when you're finished with her hair, and she likes what she sees," Kenneth explained.

Whether it was traveling with Judy Garland for her dynamic personal appearances and being credited as her hairdresser backstage, or working with Marilyn Monroe and seeing his photograph printed in countless newspapers across the United States, Kenneth was cognizant of the enormous amount of publicity he received. When one of his closest clients lived in the White House, the name Kenneth gained international exposure.

However, regardless of all that, Kenneth diluted the importance of his highly visible clients. "If we had more celebrities, it wouldn't matter if their hair didn't look better," he said. "Publicity may bring them in, but if they're not happy, they won't come back and bring their friends. Eighty-five percent of the clients don't come here because of the celebrities. I must say it's exciting to have the names and meet the people who are celebrities and to make them look better."

Never the one to turn down clients, he respected everyone, whether they would be young career ladies, teenagers, or suburban housewives. Celebrity was merely a form of stimulating business to Kenneth—highly visible people had waited while he cut a secretary's hair. He would cut anybody's hair. At least once. For anytime after, he would pass them on to others from his staff, or else they would have always requested him.

Kenneth continued, "Some women come to me three times a week. Some come only twice a year. Some come every six weeks for a haircut. And I have many transient clients, people who visit New York City once a year and want to have a marvelous time. Part of their trip is a trip to Kenneth's."

Creating gossip never interested him, a philosophy he had started at Helena Rubinstein's salon, whether he was directly involved or not. If anyone in his presence began gossiping about others, he was known to quietly walk away. It was a behavior that very much contributed to his success. For decades, he had been approached countless times to write a tell-all memoir.

Journalists would show up, asking what was the latest with Jacqueline Kennedy's hair. A news magazine had offered Kenneth money if he would show on a

Jean inside the wrought iron doors

Kenneth welcomes her from the yellow and black stairway

Chandeliered paisley drying tent

Porthault towels in bamboo case
Parquet-floored exercise room

Ravishingly turbaned for a sauna

Make-up room, theater-watt mirror lights

One of a dozen flower patterns
the eye gathers up

In the blue room, deciding
how to style Jean's hair

Jean's long signature bangs softly
brushed by Kenneth; rest of
hair slightly swirled up at the tips

Marble and gilt dome drying room
Kenneth's room—antiques, a mimosa tree

Drying out on a red chaise longue
Setting salon, art nouveau, potted palms

Glamour, July 1963.

model how he cut the first lady's hair. The *New York Times* called to confirm whether or not the rumors were true that her hair was going to be cut. As he remained tight lipped, gossip newspapers would pay the staff to tip them when Jacqueline was in the salon.

Kenneth had almost gone into forbidden territory, but he quickly learned his lesson. "You have to know enough not to get carried away," he shared. "You have to know enough not to misuse your association with your clients. You can make terrible mistakes. You know, I almost did. When Jackie was in the White House, I allowed *Glamour* magazine, which was doing a big story on me, to photograph me going through the White House gates. I was too stupid to understand that this could be offensive to Mrs. Kennedy."

The salon was devoid of rumors or mindless chatter, having only an atmosphere of luxury and repose. "Kenneth's house seems to have a curiously hypnotic effect on most women," *Vogue* once stated. "The décor, the ambiance, the techniques of treatment . . . combine to calm and soothe in a way that might well be studied by the makers of Miltown [a tranquilizer]."

Jacqueline Kennedy's sister, Lee Radziwill, echoed the feeling when she said, "Kenneth's salon had a great serenity. It has been compared to a club, but it was so much more comforting than that."

"It was always very elegant. It was quiet," echoed Nancy Kissinger. "You didn't have to listen to any loud music, thank God. You could have anything you wanted, and it was just delightful."

Kenneth had revolutionized the beauty parlor, providing a refuge devoted to ladies and their desire to feel beautiful. "Women used to come in just to sit and have lunch, or leaf through magazines. We had *Country Life*, *Publisher's Weekly*, *Atlantic*—but never any scandal papers. Or they'd nap on a chaise. You see, Kenneth—I'm talking about the entity, not me—belonged to them. They felt safe, even more sheltered than at home," Kenneth stated.

"If you ever wanted to learn who was in town—[Countess] Jacqueline de Ribes, Marella Agnelli—all you'd have to do is check in at Kenneth," Grace Mirabella said.

If clients were shopping in the neighborhood, they would make a stop to drop off their packages and return to their social affairs. Afterward, they would go back for a cup of tea and retrieve their belongings.

Kenneth explained, "I wanted it to be extraordinarily comfortable and spoiling. I wanted people to enjoy every minute that they were there. I wanted us to be on time instead of keeping people waiting. Just all kinds of very simple, little human things that other salons forget to do at times."

"He has magic hands—a gentle, reassuring, healing, invisible touch. From the instant Kenneth puts his fingers in your hair, you feel better, even look better. It's a kind of laying on of the hands," Alexandra Penney, former editor in chief of *Self*, observed.

"Kenneth had a gift for dealing with people like Jackie, Marilyn, and Judy Garland," a former *Vogue* editor shared. "They could trust him never to showboat or coast on their fame. His hair for Jackie

[Kennedy] was particularly brilliant because he understood how it would work with the camera—the height he gave her lengthened her head and balanced her broad cheekbones. It was a kind of grown-up exaggeration of little girls' hair. With Jackie's bouffant, Kenneth killed off the hat."

The only hat that survived unscathed from Kenneth's coiffure crusade was Jacqueline Kennedy's pillbox hat—it was the perfect size to fit a bouffant hairdo. The first lady had approached Halston, and Kenneth had asked him to create something that wouldn't disrupt Mrs. Kennedy's hair. The final result was a fashion frenzy.

Aside from always sharing positive reviews with the press, the clients showed their appreciation around Christmas. Gifts included diamond and ruby earrings, gold jewelry, Tiffany's watches, cash, cases of Scotch or bottles of fine champagne, handbags, and cologne or perfume.

He never followed the latest trends, learning to evolve with the voice of each individual client versus what was being written in the pages of magazines and newspapers. To him, the cut of the month meant there was inconsistency and no place for it in the future.

Fashion icon Babe Paley was drawn to Kenneth's cuts because he paid attention to the way hair related to one's face. He never gave exaggeration, only what was appropriate to his clients.

In the sixties, avant-garde looks and geometric cuts started seeping into society. No teasing, no updos; everything was loose and free. Whereas Vidal Sassoon was more the trendsetter, working with the fashion attitude, Kenneth was the opposite—it was the *Who's Who?* through the front door on a daily basis.

Kenneth remembered when a client came for her appointment one day; she was carrying a picture when she sat in his chair. Pointing at the photograph, she requested the same exact haircut. Kenneth had quietly put down his scissors and comb.

"Why didn't you go there? This is a Vidal Sassoon haircut."

"Because they were too booked and I had my appointment here."

He went out to the front desk and spoke to the secretary, who then called a number and made an appointment. Coming back to his room, Kenneth informed the lady, "Now they will take you. In half an hour, you have an appointment. You are going to go to Vidal Sassoon."

The disconcerted client got up from sitting, and he had said, "There's nothing to be upset about. They're ready for you. You want the same haircut; you're going to have it."

He always preferred hair to fads. "Crazes come and go; the one factor I feel is important is the cut. Even in the days of the pin curler, I realized the cut was important—nobody else did—as the set hid a multitude of sins." According to Kenneth, what was new was actually old. "Today's trends rely heavily on ideas of the past. I have seen revival after revival after revival in hair, fashion, makeup."

Not all clients heeded his advice. He once suggested to Elizabeth Taylor to slightly cut her hair, but she didn't agree at all. He explained, "I'm much too ordinary for her—I don't know any other word to use."

A craftsman who cared very much about the work he did, Kenneth never felt that he was a visionary, only a person using mere logic. He famously described his job: "What I do is only a shampoo away from being nothing."

As he continued navigating through la crème de la crème of society, Kenneth became increasingly coveted by top magazines. Whenever he disappeared from the salon, it was known that he was traveling for work. Former *Vogue* editor in chief Diana Vreeland admired his great talent, exclaiming that there was no greater hairdresser. In 1967, Kenneth traveled to Tahiti to shoot a twenty-page spread. Accompanying him on the expedition were photographer Norman Parkinson, two German models, and editor Babs Simpson.

When asked who was the single most influential stylish person dead or alive, Kenneth had answered Coco Chanel and Diana Vreeland. The admiration seemed to have been mutual with the latter, as Diana recalled the particular photo shoot in her autobiography *D.V.*: "Well, Kenneth was the hairdresser on the Tahiti trip. Some of the greatest men are hairdressers, and he's the greatest of them. So I said to him, 'The tail of a Tahitian horse may not be . . . enough. You have to fake it. It may be too skimpy. Best to take along some synthetic hair.'"

Kenneth recalled, "For inspiration, Mrs. Vreeland showed me an eighteenth-century French picture of a horse all festooned and garlanded, with a long, curly white mane and tail plaited with enormous bows. I packed loads of white and off-white DuPont hair. But when we got to Tahiti, we couldn't find a white horse

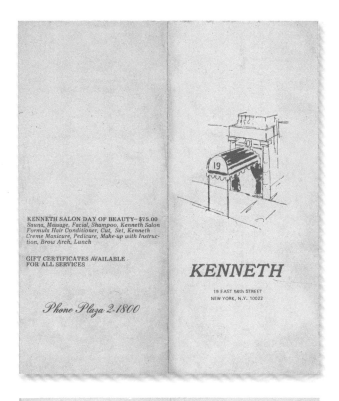

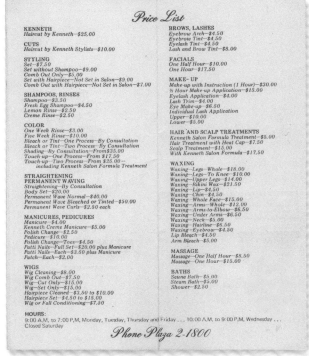

A price list from 1963, when the salon opened. A haircut with Kenneth was a mere $25.

anywhere. Finally, we located a stallion who hadn't seen a lady in eight years; he was so aroused. As I was dolling him up with fake hair, taffeta bows, and real flowers, he saw a donkey around the bend. He took off, flying toward her. All my decorations flew off, too, down the side of the mountain, where no doubt they remain today."

Realizing that Vreeland's rococo dream would be impossible, the team went in another direction. "We ended up with a picture of that donkey in a straw hat. I punched two holes in it and pulled the ears through." When Mrs. Vreeland received the pictures, she immediately sent him a telegram that read, "Too much Tahiti."

Famed fashion photographer Frank Horvat recalled from his days working for *Glamour*: "He was a civilized person, which cannot be said of other hairdressers. His role was important, because the hair had to be so and so, and not otherwise. And a wrong curl, at the time, couldn't be photoshopped. On the other hand, my responsibility was to photograph what happened, rather than what had to be prepared—and in this our roles were somewhat antagonistic.

"Of course hair has always been associated with animality, in a positive or negative sense, and fashion photographers (and fashion editors) are more or less consciously aware of this. This is also why some religions forbid women to show it. In the 1950s, the desired message was more like *everything is under control*, while in the following decades it became *now we are free* (which doesn't mean that editors, hairdressers, and photographers didn't try to control that freedom). In the absence of Photoshop, the only ones who could somehow control it were the hairdressers. Or the models when they were equipped with wigs. Natural wind was seldom reliable. Some photographers used electric fans, but that wasted a lot of film."

Kenneth, rather shy, was a creature of habit. He was known to be quite reserved and private, not one to be social with his clients or mingle at the latest event. Choosing to keep himself grounded, he spent hours in his garden or invited one of his closest friends over for dinner. His art therapy consisted of visiting museums or attending auctions. As the years passed, his love for New York City intensified. Walking the streets, he enjoyed absorbing the city's energy and visually devouring the architecture. Seeing on- and off-Broadway plays was a common affair.

Amy Greene recalled, "He was a wonderful dancer . . . he was a ballroom dancer! Milton couldn't shake a

Kenneth's circle of good friends included models, comedians, artists, and publishers such as Katharine Graham of the *Washington Post*. Here, Kenneth is seen with her daughter Lally Weymouth on the staircase at 54th Street.

leg, so Kenneth and I would go dancing two or three times a week. We'd go to El Morocco; Studio 54 still didn't exist then. Kenneth liked the Stork Club."

With the salon so popular, seeming like Grand Central Terminal, there was a memorable moment or two always happening. Once, a very frustrated Lauren Bacall needed a cab, finding with great difficulty that none were available. While standing outside trying to wave one down, she kept mumbling under her breath. When suddenly a truck driver passed by, she shouted, "Give me a lift!" He stopped and she got in the truck, and off she went.

Another time, a photographer snuck through the side door of the building and went up the back stairs, looking to take photographs of Jacqueline Kennedy. He was after Mrs. Kennedy dressed in a Kenneth robe.

Defying the crueler laws of fashion, Kenneth never went out of style. 'Though he is so strongly associated with the period of when my sister was in the White House," Lee Radziwill said, "Kenneth stayed au courant."

In 1966, Glemby appointed Kenneth as vice president, style director of their 400 beauty salons located in department stores and specialty shops across the country. Through the various channels of exposure—videos, newsletters, and training sessions—he was involved with the training and developing of their fashion image. He relinquished his skill with trustworthy perfection, all the meanwhile being an actor on a stage.

From making appearances at various beauty symposiums to promoting his cosmetics collection in department stores across the country, Kenneth was always en route. One would almost wonder how he kept up with his own agenda, whether it be business or personal. He attended Jacqueline Kennedy's birthday festivities thrown by Bunny Mellon at her home in Cape Cod. It was an intimate gathering, attended by the super elite with surnames such as Whitney, Paley, and Harriman. Aside from preparing Jacqueline for one of the White House's formal diplomatic dinners, Kenneth was also seen in Washington, DC attending the twenty-fifth anniversary celebration of the National Gallery.

Providing medical assistance to the less fortunate, the SS *Hope* traversed oceans to visit emerging countries around the world. Sometime in the 1960s, when the doctors and nurses were coming back to New York City from South America after a year away, they called the salon to ask if Kenneth would prepare the nurses before disembarking the ship to meet their husbands. Around 6 a.m., Kenneth stepped into the barge with several stylists. As he was about to take a sip of his coffee, the ground started trembling as if in an earthquake. Caught off guard and terrified for a few seconds, he was teased and reminded that he was on a moving boat. When he arrived on the SS *Hope*, the nurses came out on the deck and sang "Hello, Kenneth" to the tune of "Hello, Dolly." Excitement lingered in the air that resilient morning, the nurses elated to have the famous Kenneth come to make them look pretty. Kenneth did not charge— their hair was done for free, out of goodwill.

Always the grateful one, he once shared, "I think I've been very lucky to have had such extraordinary exposure to so many worlds. I've shared a small part of some great people's lives. I've been in some of the richest homes in the world, I've gone around the world three times for magazines, stayed in the most-luxurious hotels, been entertained by people in very high places. And I've learned marvelous things that have enriched my life."

In the early morning hours of November 21, 1963, Kenneth trimmed and brushed Jacqueline's tresses for what would be the last time during her husband's administration.

"I was sitting in the White House at 7:00 a.m. waiting to be ushered into the private quarters, and

As he opened new markets, Kenneth toured the nation speaking about the latest cosmetic products. "The openings will feature a Beauty Date with Kenneth. I'll go from city to city with makeup artists from the salon. Women will buy tickets to come to a seminar. We'll do over a woman from the audience, explaining what we are doing and why. There will be an extensive question and answer period."

President John F. Kennedy and First Lady Jacqueline Kennedy arriving in Houston, Texas, on November 21, 1963. Kenneth had styled her hair earlier that morning. By the following afternoon, she would be a widow.

the president came out—he was in a pale-gray, slightly blue suit, which was very unusual for him because he almost always wore a dark suit. He said, 'Hi, Kenneth, what are they saying about me in New York?' And then: 'John wants to ride in the helicopter with me to Andrews, but his governess won't let him.' I said, 'She probably doesn't want to have to get him dressed,' and JFK laughed, 'I think you're right—I'll dress him myself.' And off he went. A little later they took me in to do Jackie, and she told me that her hair would have to last for the whole time she was in Texas, since she wasn't going to have a hairdresser with her. Both of them that day were glowing—they looked so fit and so happy."

He continued, "I cut it before they took off so it would stay fresh."

Karlys Daly Brown, a *Glamour* editor, was with Kenneth at the salon the following morning when news of the assassination spread like wildfire. Having received the news from her assistant in the office, Karlys remembered vividly how the next moments unfolded.

"'Turn on the radio!' I had shouted. 'The president's been shot!' I remember Shirley MacLaine was there, too, and she started pounding and screaming, completely hysterical. Kenneth was at work on a customer, and he kept on sectioning and cutting, sectioning and cutting, in a daze. He was traumatized, in shock."

Kenneth's entourage of prominent clients included powerful publishers (Katharine Graham and Susan Newhouse), transportation heiresses (Charlotte Ford and her sister Anne), and eclectic recording artists (Dinah Shore after her television crossover).

"If for whatever reason one of his clients hinted at no longer being able to afford his services, he would tell her, 'You can't afford not to come,'" said former Chanel executive Kitty D'Alessio. "And he would not charge her."

His most-loyal clients started ushering in the next generation—Countess Consuelo Crespi introduced her daughter Pilar, Condé Nast doyenne Susan Newhouse converted her two sons' wives, and philanthropist Bunny Mellon made her viscountess daughter Eliza a follower. Even clients from his early days at Rubinstein's salon still came for services.

Suzanne Daché remembered, "When my father passed away, I flew from Westport to Paris, and when my mother saw me, she said, 'When you go back to New York City, go see Kenneth!' I remember when I was eleven or twelve years old, my mother told Kenneth, 'Oh, I always felt bad for her. Kenneth, do something for her hair!'"

When the salon had opened, Mrs. Kennedy was already in the White House. By the time she moved to New York City to begin her next chapter in life, Kenneth contributed to her swept-back girlish look. As the adage stated, "Kenneth and Jackie, Jackie and Kenneth—that was as big as hair could ever get."

Amy Greene recalled, "It was the day of Bobby's memorial at Saint Patrick's Cathedral, June of 1968. I had a very early sitting; I got at Kenneth's around 8:30 in the morning. I walked into the shampoo room, and I immediately saw Rose Kennedy getting her hair shampooed. I thought, 'Shut up, leave her alone. Don't interrupt.' And then I noticed that the whole time that her head is back, she's crying. CRYING. But, she is a Kennedy, and when she walks into that cathedral, she's going to look so great that no one can say anything. I learned a lesson then. She's crying, her two sons are dead, but you carry on. You have to keep it inside of you. Be proud."

"It was like walking into a private home," said Pilar Crespi, who became a client in sometime in the 1970s. "When you had a shampoo, there was a bench for your feet so you could practically lie down. I always found him warm and very gentlemanly and always interested in your life. He wasn't a great talker, and he was extremely careful. When he would cut your hair, he was so extraordinarily focused on what he was doing."

Initially Kenneth had decided along with Glemby to open the second Kenneth Salon in Chicago once the new Bergdorf Goodman, the first outside New York City, was complete. Slated to open on Michigan Avenue, Bergdorf Goodman was acquired by Neiman Marcus in 1969, and plans never materialized. A few years later, another opportunity came to light, and Kenneth took advantage.

A developer was constructing the first-ever mixed-use building in the Southeast, to be called Colony Square Complex. Anchored by a Fairmont Hotel, it boasted luxury, convenience, and comfort. There were to be shops, supposedly including Tiffany & Co., and an ice-skating rink.

Debuting as a satellite salon, Kenneth Beauty Salon of Atlanta opened at 1197 Peachtree Street, embodying the spirit of its urban setting. Decorated in a color palette of blue and white with accents of polished chrome and mirror, it retained a modern atmosphere. The styling and drying chairs were upholstered with blue ostrich-leather-patterned vinyl. The shampoo, hair color, and esthetician spaces were decorated with a sophisticated octagonal blue ceramic tile.

For the two weeks prior to the grand opening, Kenneth trained the stylists in New York City, who he had hired locally in Atlanta. He worked on-site for the first half of the month when the salon opened, and

Kenneth's fame was international. Ladies all over the world knew about Kenneth's talent with scissors, styles, and products.

then he flew down every few weeks to keep the momentum going. If he or any of the stylists from New York City visited and confirmed appointments, business would flourish. Apparently, Atlanta had been hoping for permanent full-time New York City stylists. Also contributing to the challenge, the development project didn't fully assemble as conceptualized, further reducing foot traffic. After a few years, exhausted from going back and forth, Kenneth closed the doors to his Atlanta venture.

Back in New York City, with each passing year in the 1970s, the townhouse salon slowly started losing its relevance and prestige. With feminism strongly growing, working women started having less time for beauty. Priorities had begun shifting in society.

In the summer of 1985, after over twenty years of Billy Baldwin's 500 yards of paisley and 900 yards of Indian jungle flower carpeting running wild in the salon, Kenneth decided to appoint himself as interior decorator. The rampage of colors and fabrics had become outdated. Investing over $1 million of his own money, he temporarily closed the salon for three months—from Memorial Day to sometime after Labor Day.

Once more, Kenneth turned to his affinity for the United Kingdom for inspiration, bringing the elegance and relaxed aura of an English country rose garden through his doors. It was more visually restrained than its predecessor, but he described it as "a bit of Commedia dell'arte, a bit of stage, and a bit of garden."

During design and construction, he created a men's salon with imported chairs from Italy, a barber-shop of his own, on the ground floor. Walking through the entrance and to the left of the main room, having removed the clothing and accessories boutique, Kenneth sprung up an oasis for men that included changing, cutting, and treatment rooms. He didn't believe in things being unisex—men and women should remain separated. Once upon a time, salons could service only ladies, and barbershops were to service gentlemen, and the men who came to Kenneth's, usually the husbands and sons of the salon's

female clients, were hurriedly brought up the elevator and to small rooms in different parts of the salon. They would be somewhat hidden. It worked, but it was awkward. Now things had changed.

The salon, through its metamorphosis, still retained its sense of luxury—mirror frames wrapped in a rose-print chintz, flowered wallpaper, plush upholstered chairs, cloud-painted ceilings, and a deep-emerald-green velvet roundabout banquet. It was a profusion of elegant, dainty colors. The clients loved the change; it was well-received.

Surprisingly, during the renovation one of the salon's top colorists opened his own salon on Madison Avenue. Not only did several employees follow him, but so did Jacqueline Kennedy. The press called their cold war the "salon wars."

Kenneth said, "It has nothing to do with any hairdressers at war. It may seem silly, but to me, it

waters down thirty years of time and effort." Then, continuing with Mrs. Kennedy's departure, "That's what loyalty is. The press takes the attitude that I've lost something. I've lost nothing at all."

The inevitable forces of change continued when, in the early morning hours of May 16, 1990, Kenneth received a phone call that would change his life forever, a moment that he would never quite fully recover from. His vice president, Victoria Meekins, informed him sometime past 5 a.m. that the salon was on fire.

To add to the somber mood of that horrific Wednesday, "it was raining in a way I had never seen before," Kenneth said. However, not even the heaviest deluge could battle the inferno that had started from bad electrical wiring on the second floor and engulfed 19 East 54th Street.

Kenneth's cab was forced to stop somewhere near Park Avenue and 53rd Street, and he ran the remaining city blocks. As he got closer, he saw the mob that had gathered. Mayhem flooded the House of Kenneth as every

imaginable person showed up in the midst of the barrage of fire trucks to watch the conflagration. Pedestrians, employees, clients, and longtime friends watched as their club was being reduced to ashes as over 100 firefighters battled the flames. Kenneth watched with tears in his eyes.

"And then BAM! It burnt down," fashion illustrator Joe Eula recalled.

"The fire was such a tragedy. I was on my way to work that day, and I saw all the fire engines going to 54th Street. I stayed on the sidewalk for a while, watching. It was too depressing," recalled Babs Simpson.

Reporters had moved in, looking for any piece of information that they could broadcast. "Devastating. We're like a family, the Kenneth gang," Kitty D'Alessio had shared with one of the local news channels. Hearing of the news, the competition sent spokesmen to recruit the suddenly unemployed staff.

"Nobody offered 'me' a job," Kenneth bitterly said. "I do, however, recall a girl from a daily newspaper asking, 'Kenneth, how do you feel right now?' And I replied, 'How the f*** do you think I feel? Go away!' I mean, how

does anyone expect you to 'feel' while you're watching your whole life go up in smoke?"

By the afternoon, the incineration that had started at 4:50 a.m. had been tamed and extinguished. A sixty-three-year-old Kenneth stood numb and in disbelief as reality sank in. He turned to Victoria and wryly said, "You promised me we weren't going to redecorate again."

Victoria rode to the fifth floor in a cherry picker with a few firemen to save the heart of Kenneth's salon. She gathered smoke-damaged boxes with thirty years of history, including important documents, the appointment book, media files, pictures, and his Coty Award. [*Some of these salvaged pieces were used in the writing of this book.*]

Close friend Joan Rivers refused to leave his side. Eventually Kenneth was allowed to enter his salon, the exterior still intact, but the interior reduced to cinders.

The third floor had collapsed, which had contributed to the heavy damage. While watching him quietly move about the ashes of his scorched dream, rubble and soot strewn everywhere, Joan sat on a nearby stool in the small foyer and prepared and studied scripts for *The Joan Rivers Show*.

Fearing that Kenneth's clientele might flee to his rivals, she started calling her roster of real-estate connections to find Kenneth a temporary location.

"Get me Donald Trump," Rivers told her assistant. "Get me Leonard Stern. These women are dangerous. They might forget Kenneth in two days. We need a place!"

She turned to Victoria. "We have to get him out of here," Rivers said, realizing that it was doing more harm the longer he stayed. Not wanting him to be left alone, Joan insisted that he'd get something to eat before heading home. Exhausted and drained from the day's events, the two ladies convinced Kenneth to

Destruction and ruins from the salon's fire.

cross the street to the Irish restaurant Reidy's. The trio was joined by several staff members, who had stayed in support.

Mario Buatta, the Prince of Chintz, in preparation for the launch of his latest home fragrance "The Smell of Honeysuckle" at Saks Fifth Avenue, had been trying to book an appointment that fateful day.

"All Wednesday morning I tried calling Kenneth's to get an appointment," said Buatta. Distressed that he couldn't get through to the front desk, he called Reidy's across the street. "They told me about the fire. It's horrendous. Those ladies are going to go crazy."

As the next few days passed and Kenneth got a better understanding of the scope of the damage, he soon realized that reopening or rebuilding wasn't going to be as easy as he hoped.

Although two more decades remained on his fifty-year lease, his contract stated that the property would default to the landlord if it became unsuited for operation. He also discovered that he would not receive compensation from the insurance company, which should've amounted to $2 million.

The contract stated: "In every case of total destruction of any building on said premises by fire or other casualty (meaning thereby injury or damage rendering completely untenantable two-thirds or more of the rentable area of such building), this lease and the term hereof shall terminate and expire on the date of such injury or damage . . . the Tenant shall have no claim to the proceeds of any insurance policies to be furnished by the Tenant hereunder."

"Because we were not a subchapter S corporation, I had to pay both personal tax and corporate tax on the fire-insurance money," he explained. "I could have had the house back at twenty times the rent."

When Joan Rivers had hinted at him possibly taking legal action, he responded, "I'm not going to sue. I don't live in sueland."

Sometime after, Joan, being the creative force behind everything in her life, had suggested to Kenneth, "Why don't you become the most sought-after private hairdresser in the world? Get a Rolls-Royce, and you pull up, and you do a whole new thing—Kenneth comes to your house." He looked at her without blinking. Joan had sensed that he wasn't going to be collaborative: "Well, he just stared at me for ten minutes like, 'You're the biggest fool I've ever met.'"

Rivers had gone to Kenneth in 1970 for one of his famed haircuts, but their friendship solidified sometime in 1987 after Rivers's husband committed suicide. Becoming inseparable, the pair blossomed into a beautiful friendship, and they started being each other's "plus one" to social functions in New York City. Rivers had commented at the time that "I think he enjoys watching me make a fool of myself trying desperately to fit in." When someone had said that she had given him a new life, she explained, "I didn't change Kenneth's social life. It's just that he became more visible because I'm so highly visible. He's always been invited to the right parties."

After a while, the ever-so-private Kenneth, or as Joan Rivers described as an honorable gentleman out of the Edwardian Age, started going less to events. "I don't want to become—what can I say?—Joan's walker. And I'm not putting myself or her down or saying that I don't love to go out with her. Besides, Joan's not going to make it in New York in the social swing of things if she's out with her hairdresser all the time."

Rivers stated, "If he gives you his word, that's it. The tragedy of Kenneth is that he expects the same of you. Every other word I say to him is 'grow up.'"

Almost a month after the fire, Rivers invited several friends to dinner at her home, including Kenneth. Although cautioned by Rivers before his arrival not to ask about the blaze, one friend accidentally asked how he was doing.

"Each day is worse than the next," he had replied.

Following the fire, it was rumored that he gained almost 20 pounds, and he never walked down 54th Street again. "It [the fire] was like a death," he said. "I put my heart and soul in that place for a long, long time. I loved that place. It was a major part of my life. It was what I did. It was mine. And it's gone, in every sense of the word."

Truman Capote's Black & White Ball

Known for his eccentric behavior and fabricated stories, Truman Capote, writer of the famed novel *Breakfast at Tiffany's*, had decided in the summer of 1966 that he wanted to host a party. He wanted to create his ultimate story.

Sly, cunning, and extravagant, Truman had spent a lifetime cultivating high-profile friendships and wielding power over the Park Avenue ladies. Deciding that he would need a guest of honor for his grand ball, he cleverly calculated that whoever he selected would have to be someone who wouldn't rustle the feathers of his social "swans." Solidifying his power, Katharine Graham, publisher of the *Washington Post* and *Newsweek*, had been the perfect choice. Residing in Washington, DC, she had unexpectedly and instantaneously become the most powerful woman in the United States, and Truman would use his ball to officially debut her to New York City's upper class.

With a nod to the Ascot scene, the inspiration for the ball was the movie *My Fair Lady*. Truman set his rules. Guests were to dress in either black or white and to wear a mask, which he allowed to be removed at

midnight, and any details regarding the festivities were to remain top secret. Having spent months writing and editing his guest list, Truman felt he had meticulously perfected his accomplices to his greatest plot—there would be over 500 attendees to his soiree at the Plaza Hotel's Grand Ballroom. Fashion designers were inundated with making dresses, and milliners worked around the clock to construct masks.

Although the ball commenced at 10 p.m. on November 28, preparations began well into the early morning. One of the most important accessories of the evening: hair. An abundance of it. Luxurious, silky, extravagant hair.

Kenneth and his salon were in a full frenzy that day. A steady stream of cars pulled up and away at 54th Street from opening to close: at full capacity, ladies would wait on staircases before finding an unoccupied chair. Hairdos became grand compositions of hairpieces, feathers, and jewelry. Mistresses, ex-wives, and wives were painstakingly kept away from one another. The madness had spread from within 54th Street and throughout New York City as

Along with jewels and masks, hair was the ultimate accessory. Here, filmmaker Peter Gimbel is seen with Princess Luciana Pignatelli and Countess Consuelo Crespi, who had both visited the Kenneth Salon earlier that day.

Candice Bergen and Frank Sinatra.

hadn't been deemed worthy in New York City society. It created hostility and vanity—the ripple effects reverberated for months. Truman's shrewd plan had been catapulted to legendary status. The media called it "the Party of the Century," while others labeled it as a turning point in society—going from one of exclusivity and elegance to one of ostentatious spending and social media fame.

"They published the guest list in the newspaper, and it was embarrassing to not be invited," Gloria remembered. "Truman wanted his way—he wanted only his version of the Top 400. He was wonderfully talented."

word got around of the event. Gossip column writers, paparazzi, and curious onlookers started to congregate. Once ready, the guests attended preball dinner parties at numerous homes of the elite.

As Kenneth was about to depart from the salon, finished for the day, he saw a lady sitting in a chair. She was the last client, and it was late. Noticing that she was waiting to be serviced, he stopped to talk to her.

"You know, I'm going to a party tonight, and I'm worried about time . . . actually, I'm the honoree of the party," Katharine Graham informed him. Realizing what had to be quickly done, Kenneth ran downstairs to select a hairpiece from the wig shop. He hurriedly worked her hair around the wig, styling it with volume, deciding she needed her presence amplified when she walked in.

Marella Agnelli, Diana Vreeland, Slim Keith, Brooke Astor, and the Ford sisters attended that night. Countess Consuelo Crespi was invited along with her twin sister, Gloria Schiff.

"I did go to Truman Capote's ball. What a pity it was to have a mask on and be photographed—people wouldn't be able to tell you had attended," remembered Gloria. "Halston made my mask, and it had a stick to hold. It was raining like hell that night, and it was name-dropping to the extreme. The music was great, the ladies were ravishing, and the men stayed late."

The true "grand finale" of the ball came the following day: the *New York Times* published the entire guest list, exposing who had been invited and who

The honoree of the evening, publisher of the *Washington Post*, Katharine Graham.

Socialite Gloria Schiff, sister of Countess Consuelo Crespi, had
American fashion designer Halston create her mask.

Accompanied by William and Babe Paley, Mexican socialite and fashion icon Gloria Guinness, *left*, was considered the most elegant woman in the world by New York City society.

FILM FRENZY:
VALLEY OF THE DOLLS & GAILY, GAILY

Left to right: Barbara Parkins, Sharon Tate, and Patty Duke in the wildly successful 1967 movie *Valley of the Dolls*.

Sharon Tate.

Patty Duke.

Kenneth styled Melina Mercouri for her starring role in *Gaily, Gaily*.

Kenneth styling Patty Duke before filming scenes for the movie.

DECADES OF HAIR

In the 1940s and 1950s, hairstyles were not flattering. Due to the neglect of hair care, hats were an important part of society. One style that was very popular was a bobby pin spin (take locks of hair, curl, and secure with a bobby pin). With women's liberation emerging in the '60s, Kenneth came at the right time. He was innovative and he freed hair, which gave him his own stamp on the movement.

"I believed that hair should be like fabric—light should pass through it, and you should want to put your hand in it. I thought of hair as soft, healthy, lustrous, innocent, and pretty, like a child's," Kenneth explained. The cut was more important than the style, a transformation that was like a dance: rhythmically moving around the head, sectioning pieces of hair with clips, and cutting it bluntly while wet. "I was looking to make hair fuller, to make it swing and swivel with the head."

After the right cut, quality treatment and good health are also important. Stunning hair doesn't just occur—it's the result of attentive hair care. Even so, the countless ladies who had shocking wrong hairdos always surprised him.

"Your hairdo should do something for you, make you feel pretty. It should flatter you, make the most of your hair texture, curl, and thickness," Kenneth explained. "It should suit your way of life and be comfortable. It should look like it's part of you and not a piece of abstract sculpture sitting on top of your head." Hair is meant to look like it's a part of a person; it should be decorative.

He continued: "More important than the shape of your particular face is the whole look of you. You are a combination of many things, not only a face shape, but a head size, a neck length, posture."

Gloria Steinem wrote in a 1964 issue of *Glamour* magazine that "Kenneth uses as much psychology in getting a client accustomed to a new hairdo as he does in devising it. He has gone so far as to stretch a major cutting job over months, taking off just an inch at a time."

Kenneth would at times work backward—he'd cut and style a client's hair as exaggerated as possible but then reduce it because it wasn't feasible for a lady to walk about her day looking like a page from a magazine. "I hated what razors did to hair, and I always used scissors," he says. "It just kept the hair in better condition, with more body."

He described his signature hairdo as "unfettered, uncluttered, very real, very soft." He felt that if he would've surrendered by giving clients "what she thinks she wants—pastry-chef sculptures that you can't run your fingers through without breaking a fingernail," he wouldn't have built a reputation for himself. Even during a time where hairdos were intricate, perhaps

with the use of several switches or falls, he always preferred his style to look a little undone in comparison.

Finding it displeasing, Kenneth always believed that it should never have seemed as if ladies had just come out of the beauty salon. When he started as a hairdresser, most clients wouldn't share with their families that they dyed their hair. An admirer of bouncy, free hair that looks natural, he believed that hair forced to be styled in a way that it wasn't meant to be was no longer considered hair—it was to be described as a mess. Hair: "a marvelous material which can be glorious if it's treated with respect." Hair was to look like hair; it was to seem as if it was alive.

"It should be comfortable, something you can take care of yourself after you've left the salon. This leaves out excessive teasing, hair that is lacquered into a stone, hair colors that are unbelievable," Kenneth explained. "It leaves out hair that's been tormented and mistreated until it's a mass of dry straw. Women do terrible things to their hair in the name of beauty."

To Kenneth, beautiful, luxurious hair had replaced designer clothing as a sign of personal distinction. It had become the ultimate status symbol. There was a time in the 1970s when ladies loved a lot of hair. What had once been considered somewhat of a nuisance, in the early 1900s, had suddenly become the most important fashion accessory. An abundance of hair gave ladies the feeling of beauty and luxury and being feminine. Wigs were the craze.

"New hair styles happen much less often than people think. What's often considered a new style is usually merely a variation of an old one, produced by setting or combing the hair a little differently. A truly new style comes only from a new kind of 'cut,' a rare occurrence. Hairstyles are never 'created'—in spite of what hairdressers would like you to think—they 'evolve.' They evolve right out of the recent past and will change into something else tomorrow, helped along by mechanical and technical developments."

Whenever he reflected on his career, Kenneth described it as a time of great excitement and inspiration. It was an era of evolution, where styles—whether it be design, fashion, or music—were frequently being challenged and new ideas were surfacing. "Mine was a generation of people who wanted to get through dinner without their hair falling down."

Although he credited *Vogue* and *Harper's Bazaar* for his vision with shaping and proportion, he never

headlines by Kenneth

Many of my clients bought quite expensive hairpieces a couple of years ago when falls were so fashionable. The way they wore their falls now makes their heads look too big and therefore old-fashioned. At the same time, having made the investment and perhaps not having the best hair themselves, they don't want to give up their hairpieces and lose the look of luxurious hair that a fall helped them achieve.

They don't have to.

All they must do is realize that the look of heads has gotten smaller. Their falls can be used to enhance the smaller head look but they must be used in a different way. For example, where before you may have attached your fall near your hairline, you should think now of placing it much farther back. This allows for your own hair to be sleeked back enough to see your natural head shape. The extra hair does not create excessive height or width and tends to look much realer and gives a better proportion. With some bulk in the back, you don't need the height or width at the front.

The hairpiece I'm showing you today is what we call the million-dollar mane. It's very long—about 24 inches—but you can achieve the same effect with a shorter one. This mane is made on a very small base, about the size of a silver dollar, so there's no bulk or width at the point of attachment. If you're using a fall with a bigger base, don't set it all the way up to the base so that too much bulk is created.

A fall of this kind can be used as a braid, can fall loosely if it's kept well back from the face, or made into a figure 8 and worn lengthwise or widthwise at the back of the head.

The larger drawing shows the hair worn in a lengthwise figure 8. In the other, the long braid is used this way: pull your own hair back and into a French twist. Then pin the braid at the top and also to the twist all the way down the back, giving the effect of French braiding. This, of course, holds the braid securely and makes it look much more like your own hair. Besides, it's a very neat finish.

headlines by Kenneth

Decorating for Christmas is something we all love to do, but I'd like to issue a warning if you are planning to decorate your hair as well as your house. The secret of decorating tastefully lies in discretion. Never overdo it. Too often I've seen women put something in their hair—three big fake holly leaves or a Christmas flower or a brooch that wasn't designed for the hair—and just look funny. My suggestion is: when you're all dressed and ready to go, stand in front of a full-length mirror and decide what you don't need. I think this is a particularly good rule for the head and face, though it's definitely helpful for the rest of one's self as well.

Most of us have a tendency to be a little too creative. Every so often when I'm working editorially for a fashion magazine, when we're getting the models ready for photography, we'll pick up a piece of dazzling jewelry or a fresh flower and think, wouldn't this look just too marvelous in a girl's hair. Most of the time we end up taking it out because it's just too much.

But some decoration can be attractive, especially this year, with the serious look fashion has assumed and with the no-hairdo that seems best right now. Often a woman needs a lift, especially in the evening.

My personal feeling is that jewelry is bad news in the hair, unless it's designed for it and then sometimes I wonder. If you wear a chignon, it can look great with decorated pins in it. In Italy this fall, many collections showed such pins inspired by Japanese hairpins.

Whatever you do, it should have a quality of ingenuousness—perhaps a small daisy chain around the head. Or, to be not quite so esoteric, a little bow barrette made of hair.

For gala evenings, there are little triangular kerchiefs made of gold chain or rhinestones. There are braids embedded with colored beads or jet or crystal to be used in the hair or just around the forehead.

Sometimes braiding ribbon into your own long hair or into an added braid is a lovely touch.

If you use flowers in the hair, they should be a soft kind of flower—maybe a carnation or a bachelor button or a colored daisy—never a stiff one. Perhaps you might tuck it in the hair over the ear.

Never be complicated. Big fancy arrangements are quite passe, both for hairdos and decoration. They're not only aging but just plain appalling.

Kenneth's weekly advice column on hair was syndicated throughout the United States.

considered hairdressing a form of art. He instead always felt that it was a high craft. "I'm not downplaying it—I think it is wrong to be ashamed of being a craftsman. The word 'art' is kicked around far too widely these days—it just gives people carte blanche to behave badly." In an industry besieged by gaudy, poor-quality hairdressing, Kenneth hoped that he had contributed style and credibility instead.

Publicly, and comfortably, he always called himself a servant, which used to prompt other hairdressers to send angry letters whenever he'd title himself as such in newspapers or magazines. Coddling the client was imperative; it was the utmost important part of being in the service industry. However, young people were never exposed to good manners, and "the hairdresser is certainly an artist to an extent," he said. "But he is a servant. That word doesn't scare me at all."

"It's very American to turn things into art," he explained. "That's hype. But I never got carried away with the flamboyance of the art of it all—the way Alexandre did, for instance. He thinks he's an artist, and if you think of French hairdressing through the centuries as great art, then you would have to say he's right.

headlines by Kenneth

Everybody's all stirred up these days about skirt lengths—will they go long or won't they? I can't predict what will happen, but I rather think there'll be just one more skirt length to choose from. One thing's for sure, though: there is a new "fashion mood" developing, a sense of romantic, delicate beauty, and hair and makeup are certainly affected by it.

I call my latest collection of hairstyles "Bauhaus 70," and it reflects this revival of a romantic mood. The hair is medium to long (chin length to shoulder), and there is much more curl or wave to it than we've been used to. I think it's one of the prettiest and most flattering hairdos you can wear, but it does demand more care and upkeep than the swinging styles.

The head shape is still rather small, quite visible and real, though there is some volume. You'll need more frequent setting, and perhaps some kind of permanent to help maintain the wave and curl. The curling iron can be a big help but stay away from a lot of hair spray. The hair should look loose and free.

Instead of setting the hair on big rollers, you must use a much smaller roller for the Bauhaus look, perhaps one-half-inch diameter, so that when the hair is combed out it falls in smaller waves that start fairly close to the scalp.

It may be worn very loose and soft all over the head, or perhaps gently caught at the nape in a tiny chignon of your own (as shown), or you can add a small decorative kind of hairpiece. You might try a braided figure eight or a switch of hair made into a coil and entwined with some ribbon.

The veil matches the smoky mysterious look that makup is starting to take on. Eye makeup is no longer so defined, but looks more smudged. No eye liner, but gray or brown or pink color around the eyes—sometimes *all* the way around.

Eyebrows are less heavy and there's lots of pink on the face. When you wear this hairstyle, the lips should be wet and shiny.

But there's no question he's the great French coiffeur of our time, complete with Marie-Antoinette attitude."

Kenneth respected Vidal Sassoon's idea of creating a successful training program that groomed hairdressers to be polished haircutters. Sassoon had taken the spirit of the 1960s and morphed it into a very precise cut. "The quality of hairdressing increased worldwide; however, it also took away a willingness to learn beyond a pattern. People become afraid to make a mistake—often the best ideas come from mistakes."

Modestly, Kenneth didn't believe that he had been a part of the revolution that made hair important. If so, it definitely hadn't been something that he had ambitiously planned. To him, he was just being who he was and always had been—a man who wore suits and neckties to work and had strong opinions of how a salon should function, whether it be his or someone else's.

He felt a disconnect with the hair industry, having once attended a hair show but later reconsidering, citing irrelevant material to what he did every day at work. Finding it appalling, he sometimes realized nothing had changed in decades.

Yearning to be different from the rest, he explained, "Many businesses open on the wrong premise—they get some customers and bad hair posters and call themselves the salon of the future. I have never set out to do that. I wanted to create a place where people would feel comfortable, feel attractive, get waited on hand and foot. I have always wanted to provide the strongest hair service around."

Although his success was attributed to creating the bouffant, Kenneth didn't agree. According to him, the hairdo wasn't an invention, but an evolution of style.

Armed with a repertoire of rather classic hairdos, nothing radical or contrived, he preferred not to categorize all his ladies under one favorite hairstyle. His belief was that every lady had her own unique look. "I've never been known for up-to-the-minute styles, but rather for up-to-the-minute clients. By that I mean that real hair fashion comes from what women wear on their heads—they are the final authorities."

Just as easy it is to find a look that complements one's individuality, it's also easy to fall into the trap of staying with the same style for a lifetime. He admired Jacqueline Kennedy's look; her hairstyle gradually changed, but it was never drastic. It was an evolution.

"Women get into trouble when they are bored. They see a face and hair in a magazine and think it's

terrific. They get it done, and that's when everything goes down the drain." Always analyzing and taking into consideration a client's overall look, Kenneth encouraged new ideas and risks—sometimes suggesting, never insisting—styles that would better suit a lady versus one he didn't think they'd be happy with. Customer satisfaction was always his greatest accomplishment—it was important that after he had finished with a client, she felt more attractive and individual.

"You learn that there is originality, but it is rare. The most-wonderful-looking people in the world change but do not make themselves into anyone else, ever. This could be a great lesson for people who are always running around trying to change themselves—looking for that one hairstyle that will change their lives."

Proving to be more relevant today than before, Kenneth found that people often used the excuse of being busy to look less polished publicly. Mystery no longer existed. It had disappeared from fashion, homes, and how people conducted themselves socially.

He took important principles of any relationship and applied it to his job—listening and being honest. "Many people come to me thinking they are going to get the magic ball or the cut to change their lives. I set them straight right away! The worst thing a client can say is 'You're the expert; do whatever you want.' What do I know? I need to know where and how they live, what they do, what they don't want to do, the best and worst haircut they ever had—these are the basic questions I ask before proceeding. Then, perhaps, armed with that information and the type of hair they have, I can proceed to give them what's best by making them feel happy and letting them like themselves."

The key to longevity was consistency and knowing one's craft. "My attitude about hair hasn't changed," Kenneth explained. "I still section hair a certain way. In hair, as in clothes, there are certain classic shapes. For instance, there's the chin-length bob. From that, you can make a number of variations—longer in the back, layered, bangs, no bangs—you can get twenty-five hairstyles or more."

Having built a following for his soft, voluminous, feminine hairdos, Kenneth separated fact from fiction. While the industry at the time had the image of being grandiose and exaggerated, he didn't agree with it. "I think it's a service business. People come to Kenneth—this isn't, I hope, as vain as it sounds—because they think Kenneth can do something for them. Usually

they're pleased. I hope it's because something has been done for them. But sometimes, right after I've cut their hair, when it's just lying there wet, they'll say, 'It looks better already.' This business is in part illusion. You have to feel what people expect you to be, and then be it."

On June 24, 1968, Kenneth celebrated his twentieth anniversary as a hairdresser with an occasion featuring a staged hair and make-up fashion show attended by visiting and local press. At a filming studio on the west side of Manhattan, he recreated the facade of the first two floors of his townhouse salon, including the windows and 54th Street. Nine models exhibited his signature hairstyles and the latest cosmetic trends. One window on the facade was a screen that displayed slides of various hairstyles, starting with the ancient Sumerians and continuing on to 1968, with the last ten

KENNETH
BEAUTY SALONS & PRODUCTS, INC.

EXECUTIVE OFFICES
660 MADISON AVENUE
NEW YORK, NEW YORK 10021

SALON & BOUTIQUE
19 EAST 54TH STREET
NEW YORK, NEW YORK 10022

IT GIVES ME GREAT PLEASURE TO INVITE YOU TO A VERY
SPECIAL OCCASION ON JUNE 24, 1968 AT 11:00 P.M.
AT 535 WEST 24TH STREET IN NEW YORK CITY. I AM
PRESENTING THE FIRST COMPLETE HAIR FASHION SHOW I
HAVE EVER GIVEN.

1968 MARKS MY TWENTIETH ANNIVERSARY AS A HAIRDRESSER.
ON THIS EVENING I WOULD ALSO LIKE TO SHARE WITH YOU
SOME OF THE MARVELOUS THINGS WHICH HAVE HAPPENED TO
ME DURING THE YEARS. THESE ARE SOME OF THE HAPPENINGS
WHICH I WOULD HAVE PUT IN A BOOK -- THE BOOK I CAN
NEVER WRITE.

IF YOU DESIRE TRANSPORTATION, BUSES WILL BE LEAVING
FROM DELMONICO'S HOTEL, 59TH STREET AND PARK AVENUE
AT 10:30 P.M. THAT EVENING.

THANK YOU FOR ALL THE WONDERFUL SUPPORT YOU HAVE
GIVEN ME AND I HOPE TO SEE YOU ON THE 24TH.

SINCERELY YOURS,

KENNETH BATTELLE

R.S.V.P.

years showing hairdos that he had designed for New York's top fashion magazines. Crediting much of his success to luck, hard work, and timing, Kenneth said that his work was one of evolution, not revolution. He introduced Rapunzel, a blonde with 12 feet of hair hanging from a second-floor window. She comically claimed to be his first client, perhaps still at the salon—drying. Gene Moore contributed mannequin heads decorated with mirrors, lightbulbs, and sea-shells in the form of different hairstyles.

As the 1960s tapered off, Kenneth felt that fashion had been gradually drifting, even having a lack of direction at times. In autumn of 1971, seeing that fashion had started becoming definitive once again, Kenneth interpreted the movement and envisioned hair to have a touch of allure.

"Fashion is used to create a mood, to reflect our total lives, but always to enhance our self-image." Having been an admirer of mystery, he decided hair needed to be shrouded as well. According to him, veils conveyed mystery, "leaving in its wake a haunting image." Unlike the small, fitting veils of the past, he advocated voluminous, dramatic squares of netting in black, blue, or red twisted with artistic flair. To him, wearing "a veil is a way of saying, 'I am more than I appear to be.'"

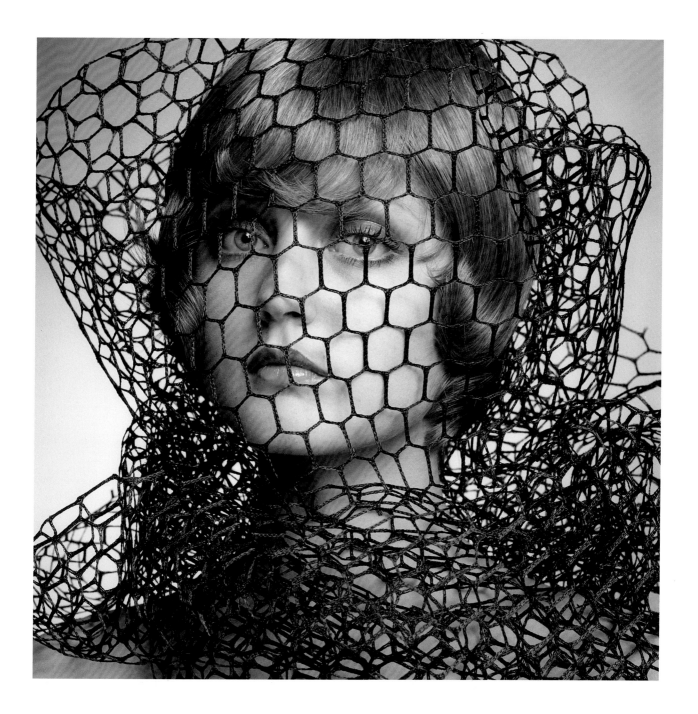

Kenneth: The Brand

As his recognition grew and his clientele expanded to international territories, Kenneth understood the need to maintain beauty outside the salon. He launched an eclectic collection of hair products, wigs, accessories, cosmetics, and a fragrance, with names like Ramu, Million Dollar Mane, and Makeup for the Bosom.

Cosmetics and Beauty Products

After testing available makeup collections, Kenneth discovered that they lacked the high quality needed to satisfy his jet-set clientele. He decided to work with a chemist, creating his own formula which was at first to be sold only within the salon. After almost two years of trial and error, consulting and evaluating, redesigning and retesting, he finally launched his unique cosmetics collection in 1966, composed of lipsticks, mascaras, and nail lacquers. The packaging morphed into attractive colors and modern, minimal lines.

The fourth floor was converted to accommodate the new venture; the gym became a hairdressing space, and the locker area evolved into a makeup room, where ladies came to have it applied by an artist or learn how to apply it themselves. Kenneth had planned for his cosmetics to take two years to gain momentum, but it was instantly popular. The demand grew across the United States, and the collection started debuting in department stores and specialty shops from coast to coast, from J. Magnin in Los Angeles to Garfinckel's in Washington, DC.

"We soon began using the makeup room to test new products. We have as clients international beauties who have tried every conceivable cosmetic. They have strong and educated opinions. They had taught us what women really wanted," Kenneth recalled.

Detesting the look of fake gold, Kenneth launched his lipstick in lacquer packages in four different colors, the mascara in a unique container, and the nail lacquers were limited to eleven shades.

"When word got around, Bergdorf Goodman asked if they could have the three items. They were very good to us and gave us considerable window space," Kenneth said.

As the collection's popularity increased, he noticed the difficulties of maintaining the momentum. Financial

Visible smoke damage from the 54th Street salon's fire can be seen
on the advertisements of Kenneth's cosmetics.

Women become Kenneth disciples because he makes them look young.

One refreshing truth is making Kenneth the leader of the cosmetic industry.

"The only reason for make-up is to make you look young." Abruptly, this relaxed credo has changed the make-up habits of America's most fashionable women.

And the extraordinary line of cosmetics that is making them look young is now available to you at your Kenneth counter.

Where you can buy Kenneth products to make you look young:

ALLENTOWN, PA.:
HESS'

ATLANTA:
RICH'S

BOSTON:
FILENE'S

BUFFALO:
ADAM, MELDRUM
& ANDERSON

CALIFORNIA:
BUFFUMS

CHICAGO:
CARSON, PIRIE, SCOTT

CINCINNATI:
GIDDING-JENNY

CLEVELAND:
HIGBEE'S

DALLAS:
SANGER HARRIS

DETROIT:
J. L. HUDSONS

FLORIDA:
BURDINES

HOUSTON:
FOLEYS

MEMPHIS:
LOWENSTEINS

MINNEAPOLIS/ST. PAUL:
DAYTON'S

NEW JERSEY:
BLOOMINGDALE'S

NEW ORLEANS:
GUS MAYER

NEW YORK:
BERGDORF GOODMAN
BLOOMINGDALE'S

NORFOLK, VA.:
RICE'S

PHILADELPHIA:
BONWIT TELLER

PITTSBURGH:
KAUFMANNS

ROCHESTER:
SIBLEY, LINDSAY & CURR

STAMFORD, CONN.:
BLOOMINGDALE'S

TOLEDO:
LAMSONS

WASHINGTON, D.C.:
JULIUS GARFINCKEL

WISCONSIN:
H. C. PRANGE

Kenneth's cosmetics and wigs counter at Bloomingdale's in New York City transformed and expanded several times over the years to accommodate the growing number of products.

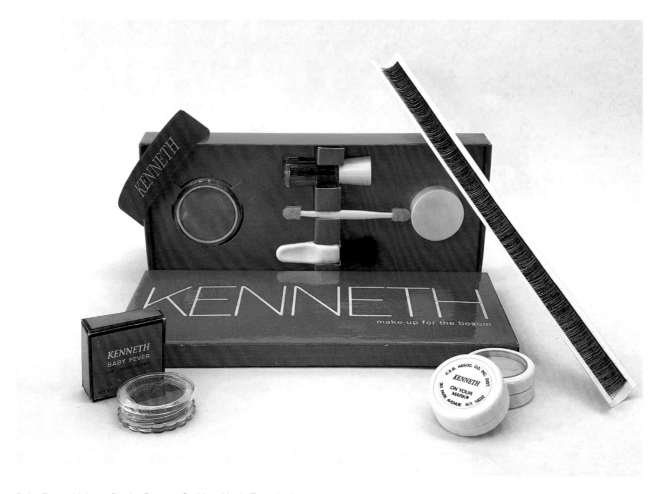

Baby Fever, Makeup for the Bosom, On Your Mark, Forty Lashes.

investments were needed to keep the staggering promotional process moving forward, but it would come at a cost of selling the cosmetics collection and losing quality control. Sometime in the 1970s, Kenneth withdrew from mass retail, eventually shuttering all of his branded counters. The following are product descriptions from official press releases.

Baby Fever

"Not a lipstick. Not a lipstain. Baby Fever is a brand new product, a color gloss that flushes the lips. Lips that look like a child's just returned from vigorous outdoor exercise—healthy, alive, and shining. Kenneth feels that on a woman, this look is very sexy and ultra-appealing. Baby Fever is applied with the fingers

(and it doesn't stain them). Kenneth believes lips should show and glow."

On Your Mark

"A rich, creamy formula in a nude shade, On Your Mark smoothens on with the fingers over any troubled spot. It blends on easily and quickly. Presto! The blemish disappears from sight."

Makeup for the Bosom

"Taking inspiration from a tradition dating to the late 18th Century . . . This is a kit of three cosmetics designed to enhance the contours of the bosom.

Read how these three cosmetics will enhance your body's natural contours.

1. THE BOSOM HIGHLIGHTER. Dip the tip of your finger into this delicate, frosted cream and rub it softly across the top of the bosom. You'll instantly perceive a delicate, youthful glow to the skin. The bosom seems to ride higher. 2. THE CLEAVAGE DELINEATOR. This gives depth to the bosom. Use the little brush to shade the inner sides of each breast, then blend until the demarcation line disappears. It should fade off just above the actual cleavage. 3. THE TIP BLUSH. This transparent gel is drawn across the tips in a circular motion. It imparts a pleasing, rosy hue.

OTHER USES FOR NUDE: The Bosom Highlighter may be massaged across the bare midriff. It also makes a marvelous highlight on the shoulders. In every case, it makes the skin seem firmer and younger. The Cleavage Delineator can be used to shade under the arms, down to the waistline. Naturally, you would only do this when wearing a dress with low-cut sides. It gives a surprising slimming effect. Another plus for the Cleavage Delineator is its use in shading the collarbones. And it can be brushed on the sides of the calves and the knees. Finally, with a bare midriff outfit, many girls brush it around the navel area. The Tip Blush may be used in and around the ear for a youthful, healthy blush. (Some girls use Tip Blush on the lobes of the ears.) Nude does for your body what other cosmetics do for your face.

NUDE, MAKEUP FOR THE BOSOM, BY KENNETH

Instructions on how to apply Kenneth's controversial Makeup for the Bosom.

Kenneth believes in artful shading and highlighting to accentuate softness and curves. To make the bosom appear higher and younger, firmer, more alluring. He does not believe in trying to conceal the bosom or in changing its shape to some strange geometric. He believes the bosom is the essence of femininity and this femininity should be heightened."

"Composed of a Bosom Highlighter for the top of the bosom. This is a frosted cream, which is applied with the fingers to lend a delicate glow to the skin, a youthful innocence. To emphasize depth of the bosom, Kenneth has included the Bosom Delineator, a shade with its own brush. It is brushed up the inner sides of each breast and carefully blended to leave no demarcation lines. For the final touch of bosom make-up, Kenneth includes a Tip Blush, a transparent, red liquid with a sponge applicator which is drawn across the tips in a circular motion to achieve glistening, rosy hue."

The press release photograph for Forty Lashes.

Forty Lashes

"A strip measuring 12" long from which lashes are cut in ones, twos, and threes and applied singly. Kenneth believes the individual lashes make the eyes look prettier and bigger. The eye has a more "open" look without the heavy shading the lashes on a strip have a tendency to give."

Nail Lacquer

"His own special formula provides an aliveness to nails, a vibrancy that gives a healthy appearance. The formula and shades have been salon-tested in the Kenneth Salon. After trying many different brands of nail polish for use in his salon, Kenneth found that many clients were asking for two shades of polish to achieve the shade they preferred. Making a study of these two-color requests, he had shades prepared of the most popular colors. He has arrived at 31 new shades."

Luxury Liquid

"This fabulous foundation comes in five shades. It gives complexions a lasting, youthful gleam that acts like bottled candlelight."

Lipstick

"Kenneth introduces a new creamy-rich lipstick designed to make lips fresh and beautiful all day. The lipstick is encased in vivid enamel cases of pink, orange, red, or yellow. The lipstick formula Kenneth has selected has been chosen after consulting with many of his clients. Each of these ladies has expressed her feeling concerning lipstick color, texture and fragrance."

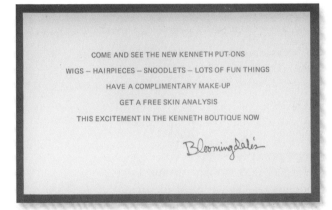

COME AND SEE THE NEW KENNETH PUT-ONS

WIGS – HAIRPIECES – SNOODLETS – LOTS OF FUN THINGS

HAVE A COMPLIMENTARY MAKE-UP

GET A FREE SKIN ANALYSIS

THIS EXCITEMENT IN THE KENNETH BOUTIQUE NOW

Bloomingdale's

Fragrance

Kenneth started formulating his own fragrance, but with an inundation of perfume notes, the process had taken longer than he had planned. The winning combination was a beautiful blend of woody vetiver, mousse de chene, patchouli, and a rich jasmine-rose floral complex. Named RAMU (which means "to love" in Sumerian, the earliest-known written language), it was marketed as "the smell of the stem just before the flower blooms—a green smell." It launched and Bergdorf Goodman immediately added it to the cosmetics collection, as did Bonwit Teller. The bottle was custom-designed in London. Kenneth owned and held on to the mold until years later, when the British company approached him to inform him that another brand was interested in the bottle. After much thought, he released the rights to the design.

Newspaper clippings of Kenneth's various wigs.

Wigs

In the 1970s, Kenneth became one of the first hair-dressers to create a wig collection when he introduced what he called his Put-Ons. "Wigs are the hats of the '70s. Like many fashion accessories, they are instant Cinderella. They are second heads for women who have collected entire wardrobes of them," Kenneth explained. "Fake hair used to be worn only out of necessity by people who were going bald. Then about 1956, a French designer showed a collection with his models wearing wigs. The idea made headlines, and before long, everyone wanted wigs."

He was convinced that wigs created fashion state-ments; they assisted in creating fantasy for an evening—they looked like real hair but behaved better. It was a way for ladies to have fun, be different, and have a change of mood. So came different lengths, colors, and styles. Effortless to put on and resistant to all of life's events, the debuting collection included four different wigs:

- *Classic Blunt*: The classic page-boy style with bangs, which was chin length with Kenneth's famous "blunt-cut" ends

- *Feathers*: A short wig with waves and swirls at the ends

- *Surf*: A short, straight wig that ends at ear tip

- *His 'N Hers*: Short and curly on top, its back and sides are long and shaggy and cling close to the head. Made for men and women.

Three hairpieces that were also introduced:

- *Quickie*: A wiglet that could either be expanded to add volume to the back of the head or shrunk to make a tight chignon, for example

- *A Brace of Braids*: Three braids in various colors

- *The Snoodlet*: A chignon encased in an ornamental hairnet made of straw

Kenneth's pièce de résistance was his Million Dollar Mane, which he introduced later on. At a length of 24 inches, the thick hairpiece was the definition of luxurious, synthetic hair. Versatile, whether it was made into a ponytail or just left to freely fall around a lady's back, it quickly became popular.

Clients took their latest purchases in lacquered

Along with Diana Vreeland, Kenneth shared the idea that hair should be abundant in order to be beautiful and luxurious. For his wig collection, Kenneth created the Million Dollar Mane.

wig boxes, created in Kenneth's signature colors of red and yellow. Making custom wigs for the salons of Elizabeth Arden, Vidal Sassoon, and Kenneth, acclaimed wig maker Raffaele Mollica explained, "Kenneth was the salon status of America."

Along with Diana Vreeland, Kenneth had an affinity for bountiful heads of hair—he was one of the first hairdressers to use falls, hairpieces. In 1973, Kenneth entered into contract with Monsanto, maker of Elura, to promote its wigs. His agreement included that he was to appear in up to twelve separate print ads, between four and eight television commercials, up to twelve television talk show appearances on behalf of Elura, and a maximum of two five-minute training films.

Kenneth's famous red-and-yellow wig boxes.

Accessories

In the fall of 1963, Kenneth launched a series of evening masks aimed for the holiday season. They were advertised "to protect makeup and preserve the complexion while going about the evening festivities. Effective too, at the theater or opera . . . they give a woman a mystique and interest that speaks of ultra-femininity." Beautifully decorated with jewels, feathers, and lacquer, the bespoke masks, whether full or half shapes, were to add a touch of elegance and allure. If needed, they could be used in the salon or at home to protect the face while hair spray was being applied.

Hair Products

Kenneth believed that hair spray was to be used lightly to control a hairdo so that hair didn't fall out of place—it was never to give the appearance of being lacquered or impenetrable. Silky hair was to always have a flirtatious bounce. To him, the perfect "salon hair spray not only keeps your hair in place but adds body without lacquer, sheen without separating, and gives your hair a delicately lovely scent without interfering with your own personal perfume."

A press release photograph for Kenneth's scarves.

The Park Avenue Years at the Waldorf Astoria Hotel

Displaced and devastated, Kenneth searched how to collect the pieces of his shattered world. Within weeks and a few blocks away on Madison Avenue, the Eva of New York salon, nestled at the Helmsley Palace Hotel, extended temporary refuge, allowing Kenneth and a fraction of his staff to rent a handful of salon chairs. The remainder of his brigade promised to return once he secured a sizeable space to accommodate them all.

Although the interior was blatantly not to Kenneth's taste—an obsolete color palette of white, beige, and gold—he was grateful. The salon went from being rather quiet to congested once Kenneth moved in.

"He was sort of double-decker there at the Helmsley," Kitty D'Alessio said. "It was a pretty tacky place."

"'I think he's got the most loyal group of people around him. I mean, where he is now, it's perfectly awful. We're squeezed in; there's no air," echoed Brooke Astor.

The Kenneth Salon stayed for approximately eighteen months. The lack of control was bothersome; the hallway had become his office. Victoria managed operations from an office rented from Bunny Mellon on 70th Street off Lexington Avenue.

"After that, like all good diplomats, he ended up at the Waldorf Astoria," Joe Eula said.

In 1992, Kenneth closed on an outdated 5,000-square-foot salon in the lobby of the landmark Waldorf Astoria Hotel. The timing had been perfect—Kenneth was looking for a new home, and the hotel was searching for the right person to breathe life into a dismal corner of the building. Within months, the negotiations were complete, and so began the next chapter.

This time, he turned to Italy for inspiration and influence. With a Palladian spirit, the salon was considerably smaller than its 17,000-square-foot predecessor on 54th Street. Real-estate prices by square feet in Manhattan had dramatically increased; space had become an ultimate luxury. Kenneth realized that he had to be sensible, that the times had changed and he needed something that would earn and produce.

"He's really stuck around," Joan Rivers said. "And it proves it was not the salon they were after. It was him. But the salon was . . . oooh, I can't wait for the new one."

While the salon was being gutted, Kenneth called on the assistance of designer Barbara Brown and architect Ervin Lemberger, who passed away midconstruction, to reimagine the space. The final result was a dynamic mix of elements. After three months of construction, in August 1992 Kenneth opened his doors at the fabled hotel.

Walking into the main artery of the salon, the expansive center atrium with its herringbone wooden floors warmly welcomed guests and connected the various rooms on both sides—ladies' styling on the left and the esthetician rooms and gentlemen's salon on the right. Rolling arches from the front to back in the room, sustained by imperial faux columns, gave the illusion of a longer space. Kenneth had initially described to Lemberger his idea with the arches, but he realized that his vision was a bit perplexing. One day while bicycling into town, he saw the Citicorp building on Lexington Avenue and used that to describe what he was imagining. A marbleized reception desk guarded antique wooden display cabinets filled with beauty products and accessories for sale.

Plastered walls painted with an inviting terra-cotta and baby-blue ceilings referencing open sky gave the sense of being outdoors at an Italian villa—all perfectly lit by warm, sunny lighting from large circular medallions. The walls, textured, were created with rag-rolling paint. Kenneth had taught the young man, who was so extremely delighted to be taught by him, how to correctly execute the technique. The labyrinth of rooms radiated the feeling of comfort and being at home. Further expanding on the sensation of being outdoors, Kenneth closed off the jungle madness of Midtown by covering the windows in the ladies' styling rooms with exquisitely realistic oil paintings of garden scenes bordered by trompe l'oeil drapes. The styling stations were composed of oval mirrors flanked by lamps and reproductions of dark antique chests contrasting the brighter walls.

Kenneth standing in the lobby of his future salon during its
construction at the Waldorf Astoria Hotel.

The staff had been tremendously reduced to a mere fifty-eight employees, down from its peak of 140. Devoid of any unnecessary noise, the salon avoided an intercom and a radio system. There was to be no background music, only as much silence as possible.

"I realize there's a whole generation of people who think that restaurants and salons aren't any good unless they're screaming with noise," Kenneth said. "But that's not something I know anything about. There has to be some place for everybody to have a little rest, and if you can have that for an hour when you get a haircut, why not?"

The Waldorf Astoria stated in their official press release: "The agreement between Kenneth and The Waldorf Astoria is the ideal marriage. Kenneth has a wide, international network of clients who are often guests of our hotel. The eminent success of the relationship between The Waldorf Astoria and Kenneth is based on a natural affinity between the two organizations. Both share a long history of exceptional service to a similar discerning client base."

By the time the 1990s arrived, the service aspect escaped salons, as people became busier and the hands of the clock dictated life. While society changed, Kenneth did not waver. Being at the Waldorf Astoria Hotel wasn't an exception. Although 301 Park Avenue was much more streamlined, "the Jewel Box," as Kenneth referred it, still retained its prominent clientele. Downsizing didn't mean that the salon

would forfeit its signature services—pampering was never compromised.

"No matter how busy it [54th Street] was, you never had any sense of that," he reminisced. "It was very calm and very quiet, to the point where we'd actually have people come in and meet their friends for lunch there. We've managed to save that here. There was a lot of history there, not only my own but of the times—Irving Penn once said to me, 'You're in the middle of history here.'"

"I have to think of 54th Street as ancient history," Kenneth once reflected. "I was very lucky to have had it, very spoiled. There had never been anything like it before, and nothing like it will ever exist again. I'm now cutting the hair of the great-granddaughters of some of my original clients. And no, I won't give names, because, amazingly and wonderfully, there are still people coming to see me who believe your name should only appear in print at birth, marriage, and death."

History and respect followed Kenneth to the Waldorf Astoria. Every September for the assembly of the United Nations in New York City, the salon filled with first ladies, prime ministers' wives, and royals to prepare for their daily meetings. When the salon at famed department store Henri Bendels was nearing its closure, a few of its staff joined the Kenneth Salon. When Hillary Clinton visited Kenneth in May 1993 for a new summer cut, the change in hairstyle landed in the fashion section of the *New York Times*. Before beginning to shoot for the movie *Bonfire of the Vanities*, Kim Cattrall had her hair done at Kenneth's.

He was amused upon reading her interview in *W* magazine. "I found that fascinating because it's a generic reference; I never think of Kenneth as me," he said. "As I don't think of myself as some kind of star, and I've never been tempted to carry on like one." In keeping up with his philosophy, Kenneth refused to raise prices. While newer celebrity hairstylists pushed to higher horizons on how much they charged, he chose to remain humble—he never went past the $200 threshold.

"Most people go to Kenneth because he represents quality," art savant Mary Boone stated. "I go also because the salon is run very efficiently. I can go in and out in a short amount of time. Leisure is not something my life permits."

In 2002, Kenneth appointed one of his most devoted stylists to the position of creative director. "I'm glad, because as I've often said, I don't want to watch myself die with my clients—although I have been asked to do dead customers. I've refused—there are professionals who specialize in that sort of thing."

Once jogging suits and jeans dominated the fashion landscape, Kenneth still saw the importance of a good haircut—beautiful hair gave people a true sense of luxury and confidence. "We have a national uniform now called Levi's," he said. "People look around and say, 'Well, gee, everybody's got the Levi's—and the crepe shirt and the good belt and the skinny body and the boots or the high heels—so what's going to make me *me*?' And then they realize that they're going to have to make their big impression from the neck up, because from the neck down it's really pretty much the same."

In 2011, Kenneth, the gentleman who created the bouffant in the 1960s and the swinging hairstyle in the 1970s, put down his scissors for the last time. Apropos to the moment, Missy Bancroft, his close friend who had helped usher him into the salon of Lilly Daché and had shared decades of memories with him, was his final client. Much to her surprise, it wasn't until he had finished that he looked at her and said, "You are my last haircut."

Kenneth retreated to his house in upstate New York to spend more time tending to his garden and live quieter days. "Nobody asks me for an autograph anymore," he once shared. "No one in Wappingers Falls, where my country house is, knows who I am. And that suits me just fine; I have never once seen my reflection when I look in the mirror—only my clients'. I liked knowing when I woke up every morning that I could make people happy."

Two years after retiring, on May 12, 2013, Kenneth, who had been a beacon of light in an era that no longer existed and whose society had slowly faded

Secrets From America's Most Famous Hairdresser

From Kenneth: surprisingly simple ways to enhance your hair's texture and shine

"**L**uxuriant hair has replaced designer clothing as a status symbol," says legendary New York stylist Kenneth, who's had plenty of status-y clients (including Marilyn Monroe, Jacqueline Onassis, and Daryl Hannah) in his 30-year career. Never trendy, he aims for understated elegance, bringing out the hidden beauty in each woman's hair with unfussy cuts, subtle color changes, and simple styling techniques. To illustrate, he and his staff created the clean-lined, classic looks here.

Kenneth surrounded by models at his salon at the Waldorf Astoria Hotel.

into the pages of many history books, had his light extinguished. He was eighty-six years old.

The Kenneth Salon at the Waldorf Astoria Hotel continued to operate for four more years without its eponymous captain. On January 10, 2015, it closed its doors forever, writing the final sentence to many glamorous chapters and a prized possession of New York City history.

Lucy Bouwman, former vitrine designer of the Kenneth Salon at the Waldorf Astoria Hotel

I always had wanted to do set design in theater, and people used to ask me if I had what it took for such a big dream. Before I came to New York, my father gave me a book, *Windows of Tiffany's*, and he told me that if I didn't make it in theater, I could do window displays.

When I finally arrived, I decided I needed to write this man Gene Moore and send him my work and ask him if I had a chance to make it in the city. If he said that I didn't have it, I would get on the next bus and leave town. I just needed his validation, so I sent him my window displays that I'd made at the Fashion Institute of Technology. This is back in the day when cell phones didn't exist, but there was the phone in the hallway.

One day, one of my roommates called me and said, "Lucy, there's an old man on the phone. He wants to talk to you, but I can't understand who he is." I had thought, *Who could it be?* "I think he said his name is Gene . . ." I ran to the phone, and he asked me how soon could he meet me. There started our friendship.

One day in 1996, I was mugged, and in the process, they took out all the money from my bank account at the ATM. I had decided to ask Gene for money. He said, "I could give you money or I could teach you to work. . . . But if I give you a job, then you'll always have that job, and you'll have more money than just the money I need to give you for what you lost. I have a job at the Waldorf Astoria for you."

It just so happened that Victoria called at that very moment that I was in his apartment, and Gene told her, "I'm going to send Lucy." I met Victoria at the Waldorf Astoria, and I remember going to the vitrine outside the front door of the Kenneth Salon in the hotel lobby. There was a pedestal, a hairbrush, and a mirror. Victoria said,

"Gene used to take the mannequin head with him, and you have to create a hairstyle but not use hair."

I slightly panicked and went back to Gene and said I didn't know if I could do it. He instructed me to start looking at pictures of his work. My first vitrine display I did for Kenneth was with eggs. Gene said that I could do something like he had done, but I would have to change it up so that it was mine and that I wasn't copying him. It had to have my own twist. So my style ended up being where my creations cascaded to the bottom of the mannequin head, whereas Gene always built his creations upward.

Kenneth then wrote to Gene Moore, saying, "I should've always known that you would have your finger on the pulse of talent. Thank you for sending Lucy."

When 9/11 happened, I went to Kenneth and told him that I had to leave New York, that there was no work for me, and, sadly, I had to give up his job as well. Kenneth had said, "No, you don't need to give up this job. You will come back to New York; I know you will. How many mannequin heads do you have?" I had answered that I had three of them. "What I want you to do is decorate three heads, and I'll keep them and put them in rotation, and by the time I get to the third one, you'll be coming back to New York." Sure enough, Kenneth was right. I did return by the time the third mannequin had been in use. He had such foresight.

I remember that once for one of my vitrine displays, Kenneth asked me where I had found one of the materials I had used. When I had told him on Canal Street, he asked where that was located. I remember I had looked at him confused. I explained that it was downtown.

He said, "Is it below such and such street? I don't pass such and such a street because I'll get the bends. And I don't pass such and such a street because I'll get a nosebleed." I thought that was so funny. I remember thinking how could anybody live in this city and not just travel the span? That was old New York City, though.

Kenneth gave me a great opportunity, I will always say, and no matter how many times I would try to leave, he would always tell me, "Just one more time." It turned out to be the longest job I ever had. When it finally ended, it was done so unceremoniously with the closing of the salon. It just ceased abruptly.

It was so incredible when the salon was there; we would go right in and I would see him in his room. I remember thinking, "Now I'm in New York. That's magic. That's THE Kenneth."

The Kenneth Club

His love of beauty, his innate taste, his sense of style, his friendship—once experienced was to be forever cherished and trusted.
—Gloria Vanderbilt

Brooke Astor
Slim Keith
Rosalind Russell
Faye Dunaway
Carrie Donovan
Katharine Hepburn
Ann Woodward
Lucille Ball
Anne McSweeney
Alexandra Penney
Evelyn Lauder
Phyllis Newman
Dixie Carter
Gwen Verdon
Pamela Harriman
Angie Dickinson
Eunice Kennedy Shriver
Jan Cowles
Tammy Grimes
Pauline Tourre Shipman
Claire Trevor
Charlotte Ford
Anne Ford
Countess Consuelo Crespi
Grace Kelly
Rhonda Fleming
June Allyson
Noreen Drexel
Ava Gardner
Edie Adams
Maria Cole

Barbara Sinatra
Suzanne Pleshette
Rosalynn Carter
Sheila MacRae
Princess Luciana Pignatelli
Marilyn Monroe
Karen Graham
Shirley MacLaine
Countess Christina Paolozzi
Joan Kennedy
Ethel Kennedy
Wallis Simpson
Judith Peabody
Marion Javits
Dinah Shore
Joan Collins
Arlene Dahl
Eileen Brennan
Blythe Danner
D. D. Ryan
Denise Bouché
Carol Channing
Barbara Bel Geddes
Betty Furness
Katharine Graham
Babe Paley
Diana Phipps
Barbara Feldon
Lee Krasner
Joanne Woodward

Patty Duke
Diana Vreeland
Jacqueline Kennedy
Elizabeth Ashley
Ivana Trump
Cheryl Tiegs
C. Z. Guest
Cornelia Guest
Darryl Hannah
Gloria Guinness
Dolores Guinness
Mary McFadden
Monique Chevalier
Mary Wells Lawrence
Countess Jacqueline de Ribes
Marella Agnelli
Gillis MacGill
Hedda Hopper
Audrey Hepburn
Judy Garland
Drue Heinz
Jayne Wrightsman
Marietta Tree
Kaye Ballard
Kitty D'Alessio
Ethel Scull
Joanna Barnes
Joanne Carson
Ellin Saltzman
Susan Newhouse

Anita Colby
Candice Bergen
Lisa Fonssagrives
Arianna Huffington
Shirley Lord
Gael Love
Helen Gurley Brown
Lauren Bacall
Mollie Parnis
Bunny Mellon
Happy Rockefeller
Christina Onassis
Felicia Cohn Montealegre
Kay Kendall
Joan Rivers
Rose Kennedy
Kitty Carlisle Hart
Liza Minnelli
Eleanor Lambert
Diana Ross
Kay Thompson
Natalie Schafer
HRH Princess Lalla Nuzha of Morocco
Amy Greene
Mary Boone
Lillian Ross
Lally Weymouth
Nancy Kissinger
Caroline Kennedy
Nancy Sinatra

On September 28, 1966, Hollywood actress Ava Gardner attended
the premiere of *The Bible: In the Beginning* in New York City.

Also known as the "Waldorf of the Catskills," Grossinger's Resort attracted the jet set and the affluent. Kenneth was photographed with American actress Betty Furness in 1963.

Henry Koehler, former fashion illustrator

The illustrations were an assignment from Diana Vreeland, and I remember her saying, "Now, Henry, you must go and draw this because 'hair' is important! Hair! Hair! Hair!" She was a very flamboyant woman. I spent a week, more or less, going to the salon, and it was fascinating to me because I had never been to a lady's hair parlor, and this was the chicest one that ever was in New York. The salon was always busy, and

I was fascinated that Mrs. Vreeland got the women to model for me. She knew them all and persuaded them for me.

In those days, *Vogue* was a very handsome magazine, and I was very happy that they asked me to do that piece. Those were the days when hand-drawn illustrations were popular—photography pretty much wiped them out.

I had received a call from Mrs. Vreeland; I think because both Carl Erickson and René Bouché had died and they needed an illustrator. So I did that particular job

Illustrator Henry Koehler was commissioned by Diana Vreeland to
draw the elegance of the Kenneth Salon and its clients for a 1963
issue of *Vogue*.

of Mr. Kenneth's hair salon, and I think it was the last major of the hand-drawn illustrations they ever ran, because from then on, it was all photography. Fashion drawing, every dress and whatnot, looked better than it would in a photograph because you could exaggerate.

I was known as a sporting illustrator, but I did a lot of fashion ads for a company called Galey & Lord, which made fabric. One day, I received a call from Mr. Lord, who was the head of the company, and he asked me to go into the office and talk about projects. So I did, and he said that they wanted to run a series of ads in the *New Yorker* advertising their fabric. I remember at one point when I suggested to run it in *Women's Wear Daily*, he said that if they did it in the *New Yorker* the audience would respect it more. How the times have changed!

Grace Mirabella, former editor in chief of *Vogue*

It [54th Street] was a lovely salon, very attractive. There was a very talented group of people who worked there; I remember the ladies behind the front desk were so beautiful. Running a great business, Kenneth's work ethic was calm, firm, and so professional.

I was working under Diana Vreeland at the time, and I would go to Kenneth's around 11:30 a.m. to meet her to pick up or discuss work. Diana would leave home and go directly to the salon before going to the office, which we would ride together after she was done getting her hair done. At the time, the *Vogue* offices were at 420 Lexington Avenue, the Graybar Building next to Grand Central Terminal. I didn't realize at the time that it would next be me sitting in her chair someday.

She had asked me to work for her, and it was an opportunity impossible to turn down. I was an associate editor, but I ended up working as an assistant, which was a title I never liked. Kenneth would talk to Diana about booking whatever hairdresser from the salon for sittings (photo shoots), but Mrs. Vreeland and I agreed that we didn't want two to three hairdressers per sitting. We preferred to just have one per shoot / per day, since we didn't think it was fair to take so many hairdressers from the salon at once.

There was one sitting in particular I vaguely remember. We were in Paris and Kenneth styled the

hair. Candice Bergen was the model. Once her hair was done and the pictures were taken, Alexandre de Paris stormed in from another floor where he was styling a sitting, looked at Kenneth's work, and disapprovingly said, "American look."

When the townhouse burned down, it was a very sad moment. Between a combination of events, including thinking it was time for a more casual hairstyle, the fire in a way forced me out of the salon. I had been debating for some time whether to change places or not. Afterward, for the longest time, I had been tempted to go to the Waldorf Astoria Kenneth Salon, but I never went back.

Mia Fonssagrives-Solow, artist

I would go with my mother [model Lisa Fonssagrives] in the 1980s, when my hair started to turn white.

I remember him saying to me, "Well Mia, if you are going to go white, you MUST keep it neat along the way; otherwise you'll look like a witch!" So I obeyed!

Karlys Daly Brown, former beauty and fashion editor of *Glamour*

At the start, he was just one of a gaggle of young hairdressers available for work on editorial hair stories. He worked at the Lilly Daché Salon, which was less than a block away from [*Harper's*] *Bazaar* at 572 Madison Avenue, on the corner of 56th Street. He was always available for solving a last-minute crisis. The Daché Salon was rather garish, with a huge, round, tufted pouf in the place of honor right outside the hairstyling area.

Kenneth was quiet, gentle, and extremely talented. He worked his way up; his pre-Daché job was with Michel of Rubinstein, where one of his clients was Rose Kennedy ("She kept stuffing money into my jacket pocket and I kept returning it"). She brought in her daughter, Pat Lawford, and her to-be-famous daughter-in-law, Jacqueline Kennedy.

I remember one time, in a fit of utter madness, he bought a brace of greyhounds from Gimbel's—a store not usually associated with quality canines. The dogs proved allergic to training and demolished the flower beds in the garden of his brownstone rental apartment. So one day, when he ran into another hairdresser from the Rubinstein salon on 5th Avenue while walking them, and the latter admired the dogs, Kenneth calmly handed them over with a sigh of relief.

Kenneth began to be noticed for his masterly way of cutting hair. By the time I moved to *Glamour*, in 1956, we were great friends, and I was eager to spread word of his talent to a group of young editors poised to make *Glamour* the hottest fashion and beauty magazine of the '60s.

Glamour in the late '40s was just starting to take off under the superb editorship of Kathleen Aston Casey. She had come to *Glamour* from *Vogue* Merchandising (Grace Mirabella came from there too). When I came to *Glamour*, I told Mrs. Casey that I worked a lot with a good hairdresser named Kenneth and that she should try him. Kathleen was very busy running the magazine and didn't see the need to do so (she thought I was exaggerating about him).

Since Kenneth was about to open his own salon, he was delighted at the publicity. To him, *Glamour* was the most important magazine. Finally, Kathleen Casey broke down and went to the salon. Kenneth gave her a new hairdo and it changed her life! From then on, she did nothing but talk about how great he was. They even became great friends.

Glamour became the "how-to" fashion magazine. We appealed to young women who were now looking for jobs, who needed to know how to dress for job interviews, how to dress for work, how to dress to go from job to evening, etc. It also provided advice with the best hairdo for their look, and how to take care of it. Every hairdo shown on a beauty page had detailed directions in the back of the magazine.

I met Kenneth when I was the assistant beauty editor at *Harper's Bazaar* (1946–1955), then, initially, beauty editor and then beauty and fashion editor of *Glamour* (1955–1969). He and I remained close friends until the end.

Kenneth felt that many women were unhappy with their hair because they didn't understand it: thin, baby-fine hair could never be made to look full and thick; humidity would make curly hair even curlier; and so on. And the hairdressers at that time didn't help. There was a hair spray "gun" at each station, and hairdressers sprayed excessively and teased mightily to achieve whatever hairdo they wanted to create. Then hair was split and broken once the teasing was roughly removed.

He took endless time to cut hair (always after a shampoo); if he teased (at the time it was popular), it was done slowly and carefully and removed the same way. Hair spray would be used rarely . . . usually if it was a windy day.

So Kenneth brought hair out into the open . . . women found freedom in their swinging hair; they treated it as a new accessory.

Often I heard Kenneth starting with a new client (who had expected Kenneth to create for her with no discussion): "What do you like about your hair? Dislike? Do you care for your hair yourself? Or do you go to a hairdresser? If so, how often? Do you like the fact that your hair is curly?" Often the woman had never been asked these questions and had no idea whether her hair was thick/curly, fine/straight, or whatever.

You must realize that in those days, most models did their own hair and makeup. They would arrive at a fashion sitting "with clean hair in rollers." Mary Jane Russell, a *Bazaar* favorite, would arrive with her makeup kit and ask, "What eyebrow do you want today?"

Often, Diana Vreeland would call the Beauty Department and ask for a hairdresser if she was photographing a close-up. At times I would be asked to photograph a hairdo for the back of the book [magazine], often because there was a new product for the hair. For either instance, the hairdresser wasn't credited.

I immediately liked Kenneth because he was always on time, he was efficient, and he obviously understood his craft. Aside from that, he had a great sense of humor and shared my feelings about the mad creatures who populated the fashion and beauty industries.

"Youthquake" was the title of a fantastic party given by *Glamour* sometime in the '60s. Sammy Davis Jr. was just one of the celebrity guests, Trini Lopez was the orchestra—it made the front page of the *New York Times*! Indeed, I was in the middle of putting it together: it was at *Glamour* and so was I! I recently had a note from Eileen Ford's daughter Jamie; she remembers that I introduced her to Sammy Davis during the rehearsal for "Youthquake"—oh so long ago!

We put Kenneth on a cover, doing a model's hair: first and only time a hairdresser has been on a cover! *Glamour*'s circulation far outpulled *Vogue*, and for at least a couple of years our advertising outpulled *Vogue*. At one point, Revlon was so annoyed at all the

THE KENNETH CLUB

Women break diets, they skip exercise classes, think nothing of putting off a visit to the dentist. But cancel an appointment with her hairdresser? . . . no smart woman today would dream of it. In a word: the hairdresser has zoomed into his own. Straightening, stretching, puffing, pulling, changing the line of hair and extending the proportion of a woman's head . . . it's the hairdresser who gives every fashion its ultimate shape. Not since Marie Antoinette took her coiffeur, Léonard, on the flight to Varennes, has the hairdresser been so prized. And possibly not since the Roman Baths has there been anything quite like the hairdresser's salon—a place to meet, to see, to be seen, to unwind, to rewind; a part of everyday life.

No one has had more to do with bringing this about in America than Kenneth Battelle. A serious, unspoiled, hard-working man, with a polite but levelling wit, Kenneth has, at thirty-six, become a kind of hair psychiatrist to dozens of women—changing their looks and, in turn, their lives and careers. While not everyone who "goes to Kenneth" goes in the every-week-without-fail sense, it's probable that almost every famous female head in the world has gone or will go to see what all the talk is about. It's a part of the twentieth-century fashion experience.

For Kenneth's customers there is simply no other haircutter in the world. "The way he puts his fingers through the hair first, before he cuts, weighs it in his hand, touches the scalp," they find unique. To hair that never had body or shape—presto, he gives body and shape. In his hands, hair as wiry and unyielding as a Scotch terrier's coat has been known to swing like velvet. At a fashion-photography sitting Kenneth is adored; he is daring, inventive, sure of the limits. (This nice balance of caution and supreme confidence appears to have rubbed off somewhat on the women who come

Mrs Watson K. Blair's pale, strong hair — "best hair in this country" combed straight and round, here, by Kenneth.

DRAWINGS BY HENRY KOEHLER

publicity Kenneth was getting (not just in *Glamour*, of course) that they asked Kathleen and me (over lunch) if Kenneth would be interested in Revlon buying him out. He wasn't.

Kenneth had a house on Fire Island for a while. He and his dog would take the boat over from the mainland every weekend. Once Miki Denhof (*Glamour* art director) and I spent the weekend. I looked out into the garden, and there was Kenneth, trimming the tomato plants with his hair shears. I called Miki over to watch—Kenneth worked with the same slow care that he gave to hair!

Glamour had a firm who researched every page of every issue between two groups of readers: one group subscribed; the other bought the magazine at the newsstand. The readers were asked if they liked the page, the look of the model, the subject, etc., starting with the cover and cover lines.

The editor, art director Miki Denhof, and I would go over the research every month. And every month it became obvious that the hair pages outpulled the fashion pages in reader interest. So I was given a "Beauty Book" within the magazine every month, and much of it was devoted to hair. As I was quoted in the *New York Times* obituary on Kenneth, *Glamour*'s circulation increased when we editorialized him.

When he became well-known, I would tease him about how famous he was, and he would tell me I was carrying on, that it wasn't true. We then went up to Anchorage, Alaska, to photograph; we had lunch in a diner and I noticed two teenage girls sitting at the end of the counter. I could tell that one recognized Kenneth and nudged her friend; they both stared at us for the rest of the meal. I delighted in pointing that out.

At one time he said that he just loved the looks of Lisa Palmer, a popular *Glamour* model. I don't remember the year, but we did an entire section on her in Bermuda. He liked Cheryl Tiegs; she had great hair.

As for photographers, of course he liked Milton Greene, with whom he and I worked endlessly. We went around the world photographing young royalty, spent three weeks in Australia, and explored throughout Europe. He liked Bill Connors, who did much of my beauty photography, which involved many trips to the Caribbean.

Kenneth did my hair for over fifty years. My favorite style was a straight blunt cut. I remember that once I said to him, "I love Ingrid Bergman's hair in *For*

Whom the Bell Tolls . . . Could I have it?" He responded, "You'd have to have your hair layered; you'd need a light perm . . . all possible." So of course I had him layer my hair, had the perm, and there I was—couldn't wait for my hair to grow out!

What made Kenneth different was that he took great pride in his work and wanted to change and improve the way women thought about their hair. He wanted them to understand that each head of hair was different, that to be comfortable with your hair, you had to understand it.

Mary Jane Pool, former editor in chief of *House & Garden*

Kenneth was a gentleman and an artist. I first met him when he was working for Lilly Daché and I took a friend to him for a good haircut. I suggested she trim her bushy eyebrows. He said no, that they were a part of her personality. I admired his talent for treating each client as unique.

I remember when Babs [Simpson] turned ninety, Kenneth gave her ninety-one roses, one for each birthday and one more to grow on. Kenneth liked my hair when it started turning gray. I didn't! He suggested some bright streaks to pull the gray and the dark brown together. When it was white and I wanted color, he wasn't enthusiastic, but he told me to try on wigs to find the color that was right for me at that moment. I chose dark red, and it has been red for some years now. Thank you, Kenneth. He handled clients and hair with such respect. He was a genius.

Gloria Vanderbilt, former socialite and entrepreneur

It was in the early 1950s at the Helena Rubinstein Salon when another stylist who had been doing my hair was not available that Kenneth took his place. From then on, I was devoted to him.

When my husband, Wyatt Cooper, died suddenly of a heart attack, in grief I consulted a psychiatrist who subsequently formed an illegal partnership with his friend, an attorney, and together they conspired to rob me of my business. When Kenneth heard of this event through the press, with incredible generosity and to

Mrs. John F. MacGuigan's shell cut by Kenneth—black-suited corps assists.

to him: Kenneth customers are famously unafraid to experiment, to act on their own craving for fashion adventure.)

Now Kenneth has his own house, and what a house it is. It looms up at Nineteen East Fifty-fourth Street, off Madison Avenue, a big, old Edwardian town house which William Baldwin, the decorator, has turned into a spectacular re-creation of Brighton Pavilion, that most fantastic pleasure palace. The massive black iron fretwork doors still take a stout arm to open. The baronial proportions of the rooms, stairways and landings, the general *fin-de-siècle* lavishness of space all remain. Onto this solid luxury Baldwin has splashed a tangled opulence of Paisley on Paisley—butter yellow, vermilion, garnet red—and into it, dazzled, come the visitors: Leonard Bernstein taking a quick tour; Alan Jay Lerner; Walter Hoving poking about; a clutch of Secret Service men indicating Mrs. John Kennedy's presence. (In contrast to the colour feast, the "wet" rooms—for dye jobs, shampoos—are as antiseptic as surgeries, with shining white walls, terra-cotta basins, and charcoal-colour tiles.)

Kenneth's special lair is on the third floor. In this lovely sunlit room, with its yellow-Paisley walls, its gleaming stained-walnut floors and Régence furniture, the "club" of long-time Kenneth customers gathers. Like a surgeon in a convoy of internes, Kenneth works his way around the room; his assistants—Wayne, Miss Duval, Raymond, Gary—black-jacketed, intent, at the ready . . . "darker pins! bigger rollers!" Occasionally the moment all Kenneth customers dread arrives: Wayne pulls the outsize black leather Hermès attaché case from behind the yellow linen chaise longue: "Okay, Mr. Kenneth, it's time to go." And off they go—to a photography studio, to Washington, to do a début party in the Midwest, to Alaska to do summer snow scenes of next winter's ski clothes.

Kenneth cuts, works all over the house, but mainly it is on these "location" hops, and back in his den that he works out his ideas, gradually evolves new styles. As of this moment, here's how he sees the coiffure picture shaping up: he expects the straight, longer-at-the-sides, shorter-at-the-back cut that, in his words, "really grabbed" for summer to lead into longer, extremely simple hair for autumn; hair "swinging in the face—very sexy, much less teased for day; wildly exaggerated for evening." About this, his view is, "There are so many different kinds of hair-pieces now, women will be able to handle exaggerated coifs a bit themselves."

Kenneth no longer cuts anyone's hair in layers ("It isn't in fashion, though it may return"), but expects to go through the summer cutting hair straight in the shorter-at-the-back shell-cut. His point in cutting the uneven hemline explains itself in the wearing: when the set falls, the hair will be even all the way around. As a rule, Kenneth uses a plastic-based setting lotion heavier than the average, which accounts for some of the extra body that his customers claim their hair has after a visit to Kenneth's. His setting time averages about five minutes more than that of most hairdressers and usually involves about five more rollers. "Makes all the difference; the trick is to use just the right amount of hair, smoothly circled, with the right amount of tension over the rollers to give the set more 'spring.'" As for his small but steadily growing claque of drip-dry enthusiasts—no set for this; the line and shape is cut into the hair and a lamp dries it—Kenneth has this to say: "Nice, but you can't do it for every woman; the hair has to be just right, and it must be cut every ten days to look fresh."

If it's not hair at Kenneth's, it's physical fitness. And that all happens on the fourth (Continued on next page)

Left—in a red tent room, Mrs. Stephen Smith is combed out by one of Kenneth's star stylists, Mary Farr.

Right—the sauna, new trapping at Kenneth's.

Left—one drying room, a tent of terra-cotta Paisley.

Right—Miss Gloria Vanderbilt gives the exercises a whirl.

THE KENNETH CLUB

floor: large exercise rooms, small massage rooms, and a delicious fragrance—half fresh air, half pungent cypress—streaming from the sauna bath. This is the Finnish dry heat treatment—a few minutes in a wooden slat cell, with temperatures rising slowly from a hundred-and-forty degrees, rest periods in between, a cool shower at the end—and it's the new rave at Kenneth's. "Marvellous . . . like being in the sun all day, but without the windburn, or the tiredness—just the pleasure."

With or without such extra lures, a visit to Kenneth's is not inexpensive. An average session, with a new shaping (but not with Kenneth), shampoo, manicure, is eighteen-and-a-half dollars. If Kenneth cuts: thirty-seven-and-a-half dollars. But even here there are long-range economies: for thirty-five dollars, you may have a sauna, massage, facial, eyebrow shaping, shampoo, cut, set, and an oil manicure. For seventy-five dollars: all of this, plus make-up instruction, hair treatment, pedicure—and Kenneth himself at the scissors. The hours are slightly different from those in most salons: Kenneth's door is open from nine to seven Monday, Tuesday, Thursday, and Friday; on Wednesday, ten in the morning till nine at night (very convenient if your plans include dinner or the theatre). On Saturday, everyone has a holiday.

Kenneth's house seems to have a curiously hypnotic effect on most women: time passes—and passes. But the décor, the ambiance, the techniques of treatment (a small corps of masseuses, incidentally, works not only in perfect silence, but in utter darkness as well) combine to calm and soothe in a way that might well be studied by the makers of Miltown.

Left—the marble-columned rotunda: a small island of dryers.

Below—Pedicure with a Porthault pillow, behind a Paisley screen

Opposite—the main salon: a Brighton Pavilion

my astonishment, for a period of time when I went to his salon I was not presented with a bill until I was on my feet again.

Kenneth was a true friend, a guardian angel over Jackie Kennedy, Marilyn Monroe, and countless others who trusted him as I did. Although without him the Kenneth Salon was never the same—his spirit was very much alive—the quality of the perfection he created lived on.

Kenneth just KNEW when he touched a client's hair EXACTLY how to sensitively sculpt. Over the years, I've been photographed by many photographers, including Avedon, Horst, Cecil Beaton, Gordon Parks, and Milton Greene, and I always requested that Kenneth style my hair for the shoots. In my book *The World of Gloria Vanderbilt*, many photographs, including the one on the cover by Avedon, Kenneth styled.

Babs Simpson, former fashion editor of *Vogue*

I first met Kenneth when he was working at Daché's. Having worked many times with him, we became friends and stayed friends. Once we did a shoot in Tahiti. Diana Vreeland thought it would be lovely to have a horse with numerous bows, and Kenneth worked for hours to get the horse to look like what Diana wanted. Then suddenly the horse shook itself and the bows flew everywhere! It was such a sight.

He was a wonderful person to work with; he made everyone feel comfortable. The models loved him. His work was never grotesque—it improved what was there to begin with. I did go to the salon at the Waldorf Astoria, but it was saddening. It was such a difference from the house salon. So much smaller. I regret that I didn't call him before he passed away. Too much time had passed, and then I was going to call, but . . . Kenneth was someone in my life that I took for granted. I had tremendous respect for him both as a person as well as professionally.

Fashion in America was at its best during the wars; before, there was no competing with Paris. American designers finally had a chance. I had the good fortune to work during that time. I worked with

Diana Vreeland both at *Bazaar* and *Vogue*. I had the greatest respect for her [Vreeland]. She was one of the best editors ever. She always changed her mind but then said that she hadn't. It was tiresome, but there is no question with her quality of work.

I worked so comfortably with Kenneth, and we got along so well—there was never any drama. I worked in fashion when there was a lot of fashion. Today there is none. I'm glad I escaped this period [today]. I really loved my job, so there weren't tremendous ups and downs. I loved working with all of the photographers: Horst, Stern . . . I did many shoots with Irving Penn. I remember Anna Wintour sent me 100 daffodils when I turned 100.

There was the joy of the tremendous amount of travel with my job. My father was from Cuba and in international banking, and my mother was from New York City. I was born in Peking, and I arrived in New York City in a laundry basket. I went to China three or four times as an adult, but not to Peking. At the time there had been war, and one couldn't go into the city. Hong Kong was the farthest north I got.

In the 1950s, millinery was a big business. What Kenneth succeeded in doing was making everyone's hair look better—no teasing or anything. He gave you volume. The people Kenneth employed were professional, attractive, and great at their work.

He once told me a funny story of when he had gone out with a few friends in Chicago and had some drinks. Afterward, they went and saw someone off at the airport. Well, the next morning he woke up late, and he frantically got dressed and flew down the elevator to go to work. When he stepped out the door, it wasn't familiar at all. It didn't look like New York City! Then he realized where he was at.

Melissa Bancroft, socialite and former model

I started going to Kenneth in 1952 or 1953. I was going to Helena Rubinstein, and they gave me a bad haircut. When I returned to get Lawrence [Mrs. Kennedy's same hairdresser] to fix it, I bumped into Kenneth in the hallway. He said that he would rectify the issue.

Actress Carol Channing had Kenneth cut and style her hair before she embarked on her theatrical tour of George Bernard Shaw's *The Millionairess*.

From that moment, I never went anywhere else. We became very close friends from that day.

I remember modeling the Luis Estévez show, and the next day I wanted a change of spirit, so I met him at 7 a.m. at the salon. I used to be a hat model at Daché on 56th Street between Madison and Park, and she decided that she wanted a hair salon. Lilly asked if I knew anyone and I said Kenneth. Gillis Addison (Gillis MacGill), who was another great hat model, backed me up.

The salon at Daché was on the second floor. You entered into the main floor and made appointments, visited the coatroom, and then walked upstairs into a great open room with mirrors and several private rooms. Kenneth was so smart, gentle, and so kind.

Jean Shrimpton, former supermodel

I remember Kenneth as being kind, quiet, and refined. I also remember Babs Simpson, whom I really liked. She used to do a lot of needlework and seemed very self-contained.

Gloria Schiff, former socialite and editor of *Vogue*

I was working as a senior editor under Diana Vreeland at *Vogue*, and I put together a team consisting of Irving Penn, Kenneth, and Halston. We did the most beautiful covers, and we worked cohesively. I always think of them. It was always so fun to be with these people—they were so friendly and agreeable. I worked with Kenneth a great deal, and I loved him dearly. He never, ever, ever gossiped. Being very discreet and not wanting publicity, he was very shy.

His salon was just great, always filled with the most glamorous people. It was extremely luxurious. We were so spoiled. Everyone was very comfortable with him, being around him. During sittings [photo shoots], the models would sit there entertaining him or he would entertain them.

I loved working at *Vogue*. It was terrific working for Diana—you just never knew what she was going to say or do. Kenneth was very good with Avedon; they did a few shoots together when I was at Hearst. I remember Halston used to do wonderful hats, wonderful arrangements. Kenneth never discussed a sitting with one photographer to another. He was very secretive.

My twin sister [Countess Consuelo Crespi] just loved Kenneth. She went to his salon every day. Social life was so abundant; even walking down Park Avenue was an event. The problem occurred when Babe Paley's husband forbade her to wear her jewelry. After that, my husband got the same idea. He didn't want me wearing my engagement ring. There was a social revolution, New York City had become angry. There were gangs, and people turned on luxury; it became a war. If you wore a fur coat, you'd get some sort of negative insult.

However, Kenneth's work remained glamorous—it was exaggerated. There was more hand involved than comb; he'd manipulate hair and design it. I really loved him.

HRH Princess Margriet of the Netherlands, royalty

On our honeymoon, in 1967, in the middle of a hot summer in Brazil, I decided that my waist-long hair was more of a burden than a joy. Our itinerary was planned to end in New York, so I decided to look for a hairdresser in the Big Apple. But how do you find the hairdresser you are looking for in a city that was unknown to me? I consulted many magazines and came across a favorable review of Kenneth's salon. This clinched the challenge for me.

I made an appointment and I reappeared a different woman: a very pleased woman and—happily—my husband was enthusiastic too. A couple of years ago, I again needed the services of a hairdresser in New York City as I was planning to attend the annual Peter Stuyvesant Ball of the Netherland-America Foundation. Once more I received a very favorable recommendation—from a friend—to Kenneth's salon. Quite a coincidence and quite a pleasure!

Cornelia Guest, socialite and daughter of C. Z. Guest

I was very young but I remember going there with my mom, and it was so elegant and beautiful. All the ladies were perfectly done and put together. Kenneth was adorable; I remember I used to bring my little Jack Russell dog with me. My mother always wanted to cut my long hair and he always said no, he would just trim it a bit. He was so sweet, and, in hindsight, I think he set the stage for how women did their hair during that era. He was the "it" hairdresser.

Michael Gordon, entrepreneur and founder of Bumble and Bumble

I started my apprenticeship at Rene of Mayfair in 1966, and it was a time when Vidal Sassoon was already famous and fashion had changed. Rene of Mayfair was most likely the last grand salon of London; it was quite incredible. In those days, the clients were generally international. So if someone was going to New York, they'd recommend Kenneth's.

Rene of Mayfair used to buy several magazines, and prior to then, I had never looked at any fashion magazines. I started looking at American *Vogue* and I would flip through the pages and pictures. It was the first time

A reunion of New York's hair experts: Michael Gordon (founder of Bumble and Bumble), Kenneth, and Christiaan.

I had ever seen that the hairdresser would get credit on the pages of the fashion story. I began learning the names of the photographers and hairdressers and the one that kept coming up repeatedly was "so and so for Kenneth." In my head I was imagining this unbelievable, incredible salon where these hairdressers who worked for *Vogue* came and did regular people as well. At Rene, we didn't do that. Those hairdressers didn't do magazine work. So my vision for this House of Kenneth was something very breathtaking.

It made such a deep impression on me, that years later when I had my first salon and it kept growing, I did the same. I had editorial work credited as "so and so for Bumble and Bumble." In 2003, when we were already big, I moved to a space on 13th Street that I called the House of Bumble. We weren't chichi and didn't have chandeliers, it was very cool and modern, but it was my exposure to Kenneth's salon that influenced me to the point that I somewhat replicated it.

When I first moved to New York City in 1977, the beauty supplier took me to visit Kenneth. I had said that I had always wanted to go, and they took me. I didn't get to meet Kenneth, but I got a tour of the House of Kenneth, which was very impressive. It was another world; it was like stepping back in time.

When I decided much later to write my book *Hair Heroes*, I selected people and Kenneth was one of them. He was sort of reluctant because he seemed really shy, and he told me to meet him at the café at the Waldorf Astoria. I must say that I was quite nervous. He was very

quiet and very polite and very reserved and respectful. It was a wonderful experience; he gave me about two hours. It was sweet when I finally did the book and we did the launch party at Bumble, I invited him and he actually came. I didn't think he would come. He seemed to be enjoying himself, and people kept asking him to autograph their book. Christiaan, who is a famous Dutch hairdresser, also came.

I remember driving to work one day and hearing on the news that the House of Kenneth had caught on fire. I was terribly upset; it was horrible. Then the same thing happened to me in 1995! Similar karma there . . . he built something that was very extraordinary and special.

What I admired of Kenneth was his professionalism, his quietness, his disdain for gossip, and his strict standards. He had these very, very talented people who came and trained there and became famous on their own. There are just so many of them. It's not an accident—one doesn't just get ten hairdressers who all work for American *Vogue* by accident. It wasn't even normal in those days. Those were the days when makeup artists weren't even getting credit. Those were the Diana Vreeland days. Kenneth was the most famous American hairdresser; he raised the standards for many who followed after him, and they have something to aspire to.

Denise Duldner, former model

The first time I met Kenneth, I belonged to an agency called Mannequin, and in those days Kenneth was with Lilly Daché. Then I followed him to 54th Street, and I saw all the elegant Ladies Who Lunch: Babe Paley, C. Z. Guest, the Duchess of Windsor; they all wore beautiful suits and gloves and had fabulous bags. Kenneth had a very similar quality as Norman Norell in the sense of working hard and diligently. They were two incredible men.

I started full time with Norman Norell in the late 1960s, and Kenneth had confided that he had never met Mr. Norell, even though he had been the one to recommend Kenneth to Marilyn Monroe. The two fashion buildings on 7th Avenue were 530 and 550, where all the designers had their offices and showrooms, so you ran to shows between the two addresses. Fashion and the Garment District was truly a big business in New York City back then.

When visiting New York City, Her Royal Highness Princess Margaret of the United Kingdom would visit the Kenneth Salon prior to her social engagements.

Kenneth was a wonderful haircutter, and if he gave you a haircut, you could tell he had done it. He knew about hair, and he didn't try to do something with your hair that was impossible. I remember that when he was at the Waldorf Astoria, he said to me that he couldn't understand how a woman would pay $600 or $700 for a haircut. He couldn't get over it. We were products of the 1950s and 1960s; people didn't spend that kind of money.

The manicure girls would come around with a basket, and they would have all the nail items with a pillow and they would sit by your side. They would sometimes do ladies' nails while they were under the dryer. It was quiet; there was no music. Beautifully done. I always preferred walking up the staircase at 54th Street than taking the elevator; it was so glamorous to do so. I remember one time being under the dryer, and the woman next to me looked so familiar, so I stuck my head out to get a better look. It was Ava Gardner. She was so fabulous.

When he wanted, he could be caustic: he did not like a lot of noise. If there was ever a ruckus going on, all he had to do was stick his head out into the hallway and it would calm down real fast. When he was at the Waldorf Astoria Hotel, I remember one day we went out to lunch and he didn't want to walk down 54th Street. He was forever heartbroken.

He always had jokes to tell. He would even make himself laugh! Kenneth once told me that Marilyn Monroe surprisingly had very good taste. Also when Joan Rivers moved into her apartment, which Kenneth said looked like Versailles, she wanted him to spend the first night with her. Joan had mentioned something about being afraid of ghosts!

Polly Mellen, stylist and fashion editor of *Harper's Bazaar* and *Vogue*

The first salon Kenneth had was all red, blue, and green of this wonderful chintz. It was very much like Diana Vreeland's living room. When Kenneth switched to the Waldorf Astoria, I followed.

I loved talking to Kenneth; he had a wonderful sense of humor, very dry. Every time I went to his salon, if he was there and not on a photo shoot, we would always talk, and he was always very sure that I received the right haircut, the right treatment. He was a perfectionist, very fussy, and he had the best of the best in the business. Having surrounded himself with top people from his field, he trained so many famous hairdressers.

It was a privilege working with Diana Vreeland. A total privilege. I was exposed to remarkable taste and discipline. And friendship. And she loved Kenneth. He, too, had beautiful taste.

Mario Buatta, former interior decorator

The salon was very attractive. I had known Kenneth for years, and he was an amazing haircutter; he was incredible. He made all the ladies look terrific.

Pilar Crespi, socialite, philanthropist

My mother [Countess Consuelo Crespi] started first with Kenneth; she loved him and they got along very well. She admired him. Once in a while when I was young and I had a big event, my mother would take me to Kenneth to have my hair done. It was the maximum of luxury, and I was always so impressed by this man. He was so elegant, and so kind, and always so discreet besides being a phenomenal hairdresser. He really knew what he was doing. There was a certain regal

feeling about him. He would never talk about other clients, and we both shared a passion for dogs and gardening, which we talked a lot about. When my mother passed away, I kept going.

It was very difficult to get an appointment with him because he was always booked, but I really trusted him—he was a wonderful human being. My mother was the international correspondent of American *Vogue* in Italy; she'd always request Kenneth when she did a shoot in New York.

The colors of his salon were in tones of oranges, reds, salmons: they were very warm. One thing that I will always remember is that it was spotless. There was not one comb out of place or anything disorganized; I had never seen such great attention to detail. He also took his time. That was something I appreciated—if you had an appointment for a haircut, there would be four people in line waiting, but he would dedicate his time to you. Everything was done to please the client.

Working very meticulously, he never pushed you in one direction or other. He was very precise. The only

Coming from a family of prestige, Happy Rockefeller was catapulted into the spotlight by her husband, Nelson, who was first governor of New York and then vice president of the United States.

thing that I noticed was that when Joan Rivers would appear, they were very close friends, and I can't imagine two people more different: he would just lighten up. They had this very warm relationship.

After the fire, Kenneth never complained, and he adapted very quickly. His staff was very loyal. With the closing of the salon at the Waldorf Astoria, it was the closing of an era of hairstyling. No one will ever have again a salon like Kenneth. You can go to wonderful salons, book appointments with fantastic hairstylists, but you won't get that service. Never.

Lola Finkelstein, Glemby International

I had a friend named Lilly Berman who was a client of Kenneth's at Lilly Daché, and she said to me one day after I admired her haircut, "Why don't you try Kenneth?" So I made an appointment and after a wonderful haircut, I liked Kenneth immensely. I told my husband about him, who was chairman of Glemby International and was always interested in meeting talented hairdressers. One night, Kenneth, my husband, and I had a drink at the Drake Hotel, which was directly across the street from Daché; the two men talked quite a bit. We had several subsequent meetings, whether it was dinner or drinks. That's the genesis of the partnership.

Glemby always partnered with outstanding hairdressers in the United States and Europe. When Kenneth decided that he'd like to leave Daché and join Glemby, we talked a lot about what kind of salon he'd like. Before we decided on the building, we explored several other options, and it seemed the idea of a townhouse was most interesting. We had looked at the Regency Hotel; we looked at the Palace Hotel; there was a house on 68th Street. Once the townhouse had been selected, Kenneth went with my husband and me to the Brighton Pavilion in the United Kingdom. He wanted to show us what he had in mind, as well as to gather inspiration.

I remember going with Joan Rivers after the fire at 54th Street to look for a temporary place for Kenneth. We schlepped around the city, looking at various possibilities, but nothing had turned up. Two facts about Kenneth: he reconnected with his father as an adult and enjoyed his relationship with him, and he loved going to Serendipity in Manhattan.

Kitty D'Alessio, former president of Chanel and recruiter of Karl Lagerfeld

I met Kenneth when he began working with Michel at Helena Rubinstein. I believe Mary Farr was his assistant, and I was either a client of Carl's or Larry's, but he was in the next booth over. Michel, who was the star of the salon, used to come around and inspect everyone's hair. When Kenneth went to Lilly Daché's, I stayed with whoever was taking care of my hair at Rubinstein's. However, when he opened his own salon on 54th Street, I certainly transferred to him, and I went for years until I left New York City.

Kenneth was really fabulous, and I think one of the best haircutters that ever lived. I remember I was listening to the news that horrible morning, and when they said the Kenneth Salon was on fire—I lived at Two Sutton Place South—I ran. We were all standing in front, and it was burning. It was a wreck.

He eventually moved into the hotel [the Palace] and shared the salon with another business. All of us clients went there until he found the Waldorf Astoria; we were very loyal and appreciated everything he did. When I met him, I was at the advertising agency Norman, Craig, and Kummel, and then I became president of Chanel.

The one thing I remembered about Kenneth was his generosity. Many models went to him, but when they weren't working a lot, they wouldn't show up. He would call and say, "You haven't been in the salon lately." And they would respond, "Well, I'm not working and I can't afford it." And he would answer, "Now you cannot afford not to look good. Get in here." He did that to famous people as well as models. That was one of those quiet things that nobody knew that he did, and I found it so admirable.

Ellen Levine, former editorial director of Hearst Magazines

I first learned about Kenneth when I was running a magazine with CBS called *Women's Day*. There was a woman there, who was my second in charge, and she always had her hair done at Kenneth's. She would say to me, "You know, I go to the Kenneth Salon and it's terrific, and you should go too. They are very nice to

The Joseph P. Kennedy, Jr. Foundation

1701 K STREET, NORTHWEST, SUITE 205
WASHINGTON, D. C. 20006
(202) 331-1731

February 8, 1982

Kenneth's
19 East 54 Street
New York, NY

Dear Kenneth:

When I was at Ethel's last week, I saw
something running in the field. I thought it
was a lion - but it was Ethel!

She told me how lovely my hair looked, and
said of you, "a most gifted man who often gives
the happiest of gifts - beauty".

I am off to California with the prettiest
hair cut in Washington. Many thanks.

Sincerely,

Eunice K Shriver

Eunice Kennedy Shriver

EKS/11

Eunice Kennedy Shriver.

people, and there are people who go there from the media world." And that's how it started.

I graduated from washing my own hair to deciding to go to the salon on 54th Street. The space was gorgeous. He always did a good job—he'd cut my hair and then he'd turn me over to the men or women doing the rest of the process. He was charming, he was smart, and he was never difficult. To have my haircut with Kenneth was a way to give all the responsibility to him. I trusted him completely.

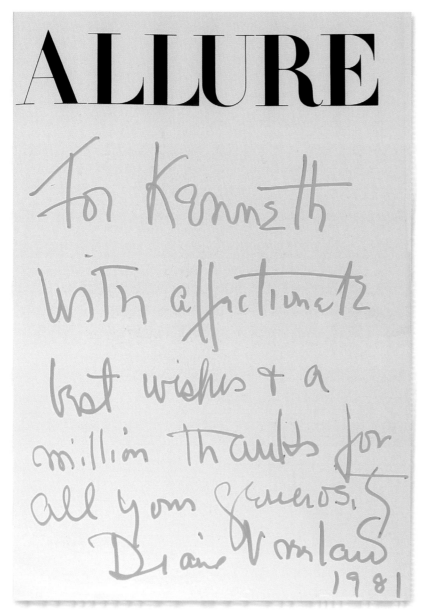

Diana Vreeland.

Bijou suit, wine and roses
Day-length dress and jacket, left,
every line so bone-simple that it
might have happened in tweed. It
happens this way instead: glit-
tered vin rosé lace, and a muffled
gleam of winey satin. By Galanos
of Whelan lace, Hurel satin.
Make-up that can hold its own in
all the dazzle: Elizabeth Arden's
Regal Glow foundation, Regal
Pink lipstick—the highlights are
built in. All: at Bonwit Teller;
Neiman-Marcus; I. Magnin.
Pearls: three superb strands, with
a stupendous diamond-capped
baroque drop that measures—at a
gasp—37mm by 27mm. From
Imperial Pearl. The coiffure, by
Arnold of Elizabeth Arden.

Long-stemmed roses, minked
In two shades of rose-cut rose velvet, right, one of the great beauties
of its time: unsleeved dress,
minked jacket—it's as simple as
that, dazzle now. By Sarmi. Bonwit Teller; Nan Duskin; I. Magnin.
Orlane's Rose Amour lipstick.
The great beauty of a coiffure—
high, wingy: by Kenneth Battelle.

BERT STERN

Vogue, October 1962.

189

BIBLIOGRAPHY

Aronson, Steven. *HYPE: The Names and Faces You Know So Well Will Never Look So Good to You Again.* New York: William Morrow, 1983, 101–135.

Aronson, Steven. "Kenneth's House Style: The Legendary Hairstylist in the Hudson Valley." *Architectural Digest* 61, no. 4 (April 2004): 212–219, 267.

Battelle, Kenneth. "Hairstyles." *Collier's 1966 Year Book: Covering the Year 1965.* New York: Crowell-Collier, 1966, 214–215.

———. "Hairstyles." *Collier's 1967 Year Book: Covering the Year 1966.* New York: Crowell-Collier, 1967, 211–214.

———. "Hairstyles." *Collier's 1968 Year Book: Covering the Year 1967.* New York: Crowell-Collier, 1968, 250.

———. "Hairstyles." *Collier's 1969 Year Book: Covering the Year 1968.* New York: Crowell-Collier, 1969, 244.

———. "Hairstyles." *Collier's 1970 Year Book: Covering the Year 1969.* New York: Crowell-Collier, 1970, 233–234.

———. "Hairstyles." *Collier's 1971 Year Book: Covering the Year 1970.* New York: Crowell-Collier, 1971, 233–234.

———. "Hairstyles." *Collier's 1973 Year Book: Covering the Year 1972.* New York: Crowell-Collier, 1972: 289.

Battelle, Kenneth, and Joan Rattner Heilman. *Kenneth's Complete Book on Hair.* New York: Doubleday, 1974.

Bender, Marilyn. *The Beautiful People.* New York: Coward-McCann, 1967.

Britton, A. G. "Kenneth Answers Male Call." *Women's Wear Daily,* April 11, 1986: 40.

Britton, A. G. "The Cutting Edge."

Collins, Amy Fine. "It Had to Be Kenneth." *Vanity Fair,* June 2003.

Collins, Amy Fine. "Truman Capote's Grandest Affair: Inside the Black-and-White Ball." *Vanity Fair,* October 2006.

Gordon, Michael. *Hair Heroes.* New York: Bumble & Bumble, 2002.

Healy, Mary. "Kenneth's Salon at the Waldorf-Astoria." *Skin, Inc.,* July–August 1993.

Jones, Jackie, and Chapin Wright. "Fire Guts Kenneth's Stylish Beauty Salon." *Newsday,* May 1990.

"Kenneth's Twelve Essential Steps." *Glamour,* July 1963.

Lawrence, Vanessa. "Hair Today, Gone Tomorrow." *W,* May 2015: 104–106.

Mayer, Martin. *All You Know Is Facts.* New York: Harper & Row, 1969.

Mead, Rebecca. "A Perfect Gentleman." *Allure,* August 2013: 180–183.

"Mr. Kenneth." *MAO MAG,* Fall 2006.

Nemy, Enid. "Enduring Style." *New York Times,* November 3, 1985.

Norwich, William. "Baby Boom Time." *Daily News,* May 18, 1990: 38.

Singer, Jules. "Mr. Kenneth: The Hair-Raising Story of the Boy from Syracuse."

Steinem, Gloria. "A Message from Mr. Kenneth." *Glamour,* July 1964: 45, 116.

Stern, Bert, and Annie Gottlieb. *The Last Sitting.* New York: William Morrow, 1982.

Van Meter, Jonathan. "Ladies' Man." Pages 62–66.

Weinstein, Fannie. "Kenneth's Clippers, and His Advice, Are Still Cutting Edge." *Detroit News, Fashion,* January 21, 1993: 1C.

PHOTO CREDITS